Slow Cooker Heaven

over 100 of the
best-ever recipes

Lorna Brash

First published in the United Kingdom in 2015 by Pavilion as
The Essential Slow Cooker Cookbook

This edition first published in the United Kingdom in 2018 by
National Trust Books
An imprint of HarperCollins Publishers
1 London Bridge Street
London SE1 9GF
www.harpercollins.co.uk

HarperCollins Publishers
Macken House, 39/40 Mayor Street Upper, Dublin 1, D01 C9W8, Ireland

A catalogue record for this book is available from the British Library.

Home economist: Lorna Brash
Photographers: Noel Murphy and Adrian Lawrence
Photo page 68: Shutterstock® Images

ISBN: 9781911358459

26 25 24 23
10 9 8

Printed and bound in India

If you would like to comment on any aspect of this book, please contact us at the above address or
national.trust@harpercollins.co.uk
National Trust publications are available at National Trust shops or online at nationaltrustbooks.co.uk

FSC
www.fsc.org

MIX
Paper | Supporting
responsible forestry
FSC™ C007454

Slow Cooker Heaven

over 100 of the best-ever recipes

Lorna Brash

National Trust

Contents

The Recipes

Introduction

No time to cook? Do you have a young family and find it hard to juggle all the demands on your time? Or have you just retired and want to spend more time on the golf course rather than in the kitchen?

The answer is simple – invest in a slow cooker!

Spend 15–20 minutes first thing in the morning, before you go to work or to play, preparing a dish, then leave the slow cooker to bubble away. When you come home, tired from your day, a meal will be ready and waiting; all you'll need to do is dish up. It's like magic...

The principle of a slow cooker is that it cooks food very slowly at a constant temperature so, even though it may be turned on for up to 10 hours, it will use approximately the same amount of electricity as a light bulb; it's very economical.

The slow cooker can be used for sweet and savoury foods: producing meltingly tender stews and casseroles or perfectly steamed puddings.

The variety of slow cookers on the market is vast. However, there are basically three different sizes:

- For a family of two – a 1.5 litre/2¾ pint slow cooker with a working capacity of 1 litre/1¾ pints.
  This is a good size for single people too.
- For a family of four – a 3.5 litre/6 pint slow cooker with a working capacity of 2.5 litres/4½ pints.
  This size also suits couples who like to eat one half of a dish and freeze the other half.
- For a family of six – a 5 litre/8¾ pint slow cooker with a working capacity of 4 litres/7 pints or a 6.5 litre/11½ pint slow cooker with a working capacity of 4.5 litres/8 pints. Again, this is a good size for anyone who wants to make a large batch and freeze individual portions.

All the recipes in this book have been tested in a 3.5 litre/6 pint slow cooker.

How do I choose a slow cooker?

- Choose the size that most suits your cooking needs — it is important when cooking any recipe that the food should fill at least half to two-thirds of the ceramic slow cooker pot to ensure even cooking. See page 9 for family sizes!
- The best and most versatile shape is the oval slow cooker. It allows you to use loaf tins, soufflé dishes and individual pudding dishes and to cook whole chickens.
- Choose a slow cooker with an indicator light to let you know when the machine is turned on.

What do I do once I have bought my slow cooker?

- Read the manufacturer's guidelines.
- Remove all the sticky labels from the outside of the machine and wash the ceramic pot in hot soapy water. Rinse and dry well and place in the base unit.
- Check to see if your slow cooker needs to be preheated before using; a few need to be preheated for 15–20 minutes. Most slow cookers heat up very quickly and should have food in the ceramic slow cooker pot before they are switched on.
- The first time you use your slow cooker there may be a slight smell of burning. This is just the machine heating element burning off any manufacturing residues – it will lessen over time. Don't worry, it will not spoil your food.
- Once you have used your slow cooker, always turn the base unit off before removing the ceramic slow cooker pot.
- Never wash the ceramic slow cooker pot or lid straight away – allow them to cool before washing them in hot soapy water. This will help prolong their life.
- Try not to lift the lid during cooking. As your food cooks, steam condenses on the lid and trickles back down into the slow cooker pot, which helps to produce a seal between the lid and the pot. This seal is broken each time you lift the lid and it takes an extra 20 minutes cooking time to regain the lost steam.
- If at the end of the cooking time you want to reduce the juices a little, simply replace the lid, turn the heat setting to high and cook for a further 30 minutes.
- If you have an unexpected visitor just when you are about to serve dinner, turn the heat setting to low; this will keep the food warm without the risk of it spoiling.
- During cooking the ceramic slow cooker pot will become very hot, so always lift it out of the base unit using oven gloves.

Choosing a heat setting

Most slow cookers have three heat settings: off, low and high. Some also have medium, warm and auto settings. As a rule, the high setting will take just over half the cooking time of the low setting when cooking dishes such as curries, tagines, stews and casseroles. Here are some general guidelines.

ON THE LOW SETTING:
- Chicken joints, such as leg portions, thighs and drumsticks.
- Chops, diced meat, mince, braises and meat and vegetable casseroles.
- Rice dishes.
- Fish dishes.

ON THE HIGH SETTING:
- Whole meat joints, such as a whole chicken, ham, leg of lamb and pheasant.
- Sweet steamed puddings and cakes.
- Pâtés.

Preparation is key

It will usually only take 15–20 minutes to prepare the ingredients for your slow cooker. This preparation time includes all the peeling, chopping, marinating, frying and boiling, before the slow cooker does all the hard work for you – the preparation is a key part of these recipes.

MEAT
- Cut meat for casseroles, curries and stews into even-sized pieces.
- Brown and caramelise the outside of the meat to get a rich, tasty flavour.
- If you are cooking larger joints of meat, such as a whole bird, place the raw meat into the slow cooker to make sure that it fills the ceramic slow cooker pot by no more than two-thirds, to allow space for all the other ingredients.
- Wash the ceramic slow cooker pot before you start the recipe.
- Once you have added your stock or sauce to the slow cooker pot, push all the meat below the surface of the liquid in order to ensure that you achieve even cooking throughout.

FISH
- Thaw frozen fish thoroughly before using.
- The low setting works well with fish and it is relatively quick to cook: make sure the fish is covered in the sauce for even cooking.
- If you are adding shellfish to the sauce, add it for the last 15–20 minutes of cooking, and cook on the high setting. (Always check that the shellfish are fresh and discard any that do not close when tapped on a work surface, or that do not open once cooked.)

PASTA
- Although pasta can be cooked in a slow cooker it is generally not as successful as cooking it in a saucepan in lightly salted boiling water.
- Small pasta shapes, such as shells, broken spaghetti and macaroni, can be added to soups before the end of the cooking time – they will take about 40–50 minutes to cook.

RICE
- Choose easy-cook rice varieties because they have been partially cooked during the manufacturing process, and some of the starch removed too, making the rice far less sticky once cooked.
- Use at least double the amount of water to rice. (However, this rule does not apply to risotto rice, where the amount of water can vary slightly each time you make the recipe; check towards the end of the cooking time and add a little more boiling water if necessary to obtain a creamy texture.)

VEGETABLES
- Surprisingly some root vegetables such as potatoes, as well as squashes and pumpkins, can take longer to cook than the meat in a slow-cooked casserole, so cut these vegetables smaller than you normally would.
- Make sure vegetables are tucked under the sauce for even cooking.

PULSES
- Soak pulses in cold water overnight. Drain and tip into a large saucepan. Cover with fresh water, bring to the boil and boil rapidly for 10–15 minutes. (Check the packet for cooking instructions.) Drain, rinse and tip into the slow cooker pot.

DAIRY PRODUCTS
- Dairy products such as cream, milk and eggs do not fare well in a slow cooker and tend to separate on cooking.
- Always choose full-fat dairy products as the fat content adds stability.
- Cream can be added to soups, or to dishes such as potato dauphinoise, for the final 15–30 minutes of cooking, just to add a creamy texture.

Finishing your dish

- To thicken or not to thicken? Because of the nature of slow cooking and the need for enough liquid to cover all the ingredients, it is often necessary to thicken stews at the end of the cooking time. This can be done in the same way as you would thicken a stew on the stove. Mix cornflour with a little cold water to make a smooth paste, stir it into the stew and heat gently until thickened.
- Browning – remember, food cooked in a slow cooker will not brown, so it is important to brown any meat before you start. Also, at the end of the cooking time the ceramic slow cooker pot can be popped under a preheated grill until the food is golden.

Adapting your own recipes

We all have favourite recipes that we like to cook for friends and family and these can easily be adapted for your slow cooker.

- Look at a similar recipe to get an idea of cooking times (remember to adapt them according to the meat you are using), liquid content and heat settings.
- Remember: a slow cooker lid produces condensation, which runs down off the lid and back into the ceramic slow cooker pot, so you will not need to use as much liquid as the traditional recipe. As a general rule, the liquid content of a dish cooked conventionally can be reduced by about half in a slow cooker. The first time you try adapting a recipe for a slow cooker, check the dish towards the end of the cooking time and add more hot liquid if necessary.
- The ingredients should at least half to two-thirds fill the ceramic slow cooker pot.

Slow cooker cleaning tips

- Always switch the base unit off before taking the ceramic slow cooker pot out of the slow cooker (use oven gloves as the pot will be hot).
- Never immerse the base unit in water. Switch off the base unit, unplug it and leave it to go completely cold. Wipe the inside with a damp soft cloth. (I try not to use any soap or detergents on the inside, just hot water.) The outside can be wiped with a damp cloth and polished with a dry soft cloth, tea towel or some kitchen paper.
- Always allow the ceramic slow cooker pot to cool before immersing it in hot soapy water. Leave it to soak for a while and then wipe away any food with a soft cloth. Although it is tempting to load the dishwasher and forget about the washing up, check the manufacturer's guidelines, as most ceramic slow cooker pots are unsuitable for dishwashers. Even if it is suitable, the pot takes up far too much space in the dishwasher, so it's easier to wash it carefully by hand. I also think this gives the pot a longer shelf life, as it is a less harsh way of cleaning it.

Soups & Starters

Chinese cabbage, meatball and noodle soup

The kids will love this one — they will even eat the cabbage!
Season to taste with light soy sauce rather than salt and pepper.

PREP: 20 minutes
COOK: 2¾ hours
HEAT SETTING: high

SERVES 6

For the meatballs
675g/1½ lb extra lean
   minced beef
2.5cm/1 inch fresh root ginger,
   peeled and finely grated
1 fat garlic clove, crushed
1 fat red chilli, deseeded and
   finely chopped
6 spring onions, trimmed and
   finely chopped
1 egg white
1 tbsp cornflour
1 tbsp seasoned rice wine

FOR THE SOUP
1 tbsp olive oil
1.4 litres/2½ pints hot light
   chicken stock
150g/5oz shiitake
   mushrooms, sliced
85g/3oz bean thread noodles
225g/8oz Chinese cabbage,
   shredded
light soy sauce to taste
sesame oil, to drizzle

Mix together all the meatball ingredients. Divide the mixture into 24 pieces. Roll into balls using wet hands. Cover and chill until ready to use.

Heat the oil in a large frying pan over a medium heat and fry the meatballs in batches until browned but not cooked all the way through. Transfer to the ceramic slow cooker pot. Pour the chicken stock into the slow cooker and add the mushrooms. Cover with the lid and cook on high for 2 hours.

Break the rice noodles in half and add to the soup with the Chinese cabbage. Stir well and cook on high for a further 30 minutes. Season to taste with the soy sauce and serve drizzled with the sesame oil.

Cook's tip

You can make your own chicken stock for this recipe if you prefer. Simply: halve a medium chicken straight down the breastbone so that the two pieces will sit alongside each other in the base of the slow cooker. Add 1 roughly chopped onion, 2 sliced carrots, 2 roughly chopped celery sticks, a couple of bay leaves, a small handful of parsley and a few sprigs of thyme. Pour over 1.25 litres/2 pints water. Cover with the lid and cook on high for 6 hours. Strain the mixture, reserving the stock. Discard the vegetables and pick the chicken meat from the bones — this can be used for sandwiches, soups, stews etc.

Pork, brandy and pistachio terrine

Homemade pâtés and terrines look difficult but are so simple to make. This terrine will keep in the fridge for up to three days.

PREP: 20 minutes, plus
    overnight chilling
COOK: 4 hours
HEAT SETTING: high

SERVES 4

175g/6oz rashers rindless streaky
    bacon
400g/14oz minced pork
55g/2oz fresh white breadcrumbs
85ml/3fl oz extra-thick
    double cream
1 medium egg white, broken
    up with a fork
4 spring onions, trimmed and
    finely chopped
55g/2oz shelled pistachio nuts
2 tbsp mixed peppercorns in
    brine, drained
1 tbsp brandy
2 tbsp fresh thyme leaves
salt and freshly ground
    black pepper
pickles, e.g. cornichons and
    silverskin onions, to serve
crusty bread or flatbread, to serve

Lay the bacon on a chopping board and stretch it with the back of a knife until doubled in size. Use it to line a 450g/1lb loaf tin, letting the bacon hang over the edge of the tin. (Check that the tin will fit into the base of your slow cooker before you start. You could use any heatproof container with the same volume.)

Mix together thoroughly the pork, breadcrumbs, cream, egg white, spring onions, pistachio nuts, peppercorns, brandy and thyme. Season with salt and pepper and spoon into the bacon-lined tin. Level the surface, pushing the mixture well into the tin. Fold any overhanging bacon over the top of the pâté, then cover with buttered greaseproof paper. Wrap the tin tightly with foil.

Put a metal cookie cutter or upturned saucer into the base of the slow cooker pot and place the pâté on the top. Carefully pour boiling water around the tin until it comes halfway up the sides. Cover with the lid and cook on high for 4 hours.

Carefully lift the tin out of the ceramic slow cooker pot using a tea towel (oven gloves are a little too thick to get a good grip). Remove the coverings and pierce the pâté with a metal skewer – the juice should run clear if it is cooked all the way through; cook for longer if not.

Allow to cool completely. Cover the pâté with a fresh piece of greaseproof paper and weigh down with a couple of tins out of your store cupboard. Chill overnight.

Serve with crisp green pickles and crusty bread or flatbread. This tastes great with the Fruit-bowl Chutney on page 242.

Spicy chicken and black bean soup with lime and coriander

There is something deliciously warming and comforting about a piping hot bowl of lightly spiced soup – the perfect antidote for a cold winter's night – and this is no exception. The lime and coriander cream complements the soup perfectly, giving it a delicious finish. This dish's roots are in Mexican cooking, and the black beans, lime and coriander are a classic combination.

PREP: 25 minutes, plus
    overnight soaking
COOK: 10 hours
HEAT SETTING: low

SERVES 4

FOR THE SOUP
150g/5½ oz dried black beans,
    soaked overnight in cold water
1 tbsp olive oil
4 skinless chicken thighs
1 large onion, roughly chopped
1 large red pepper, cored,
    deseeded and diced
2 fat garlic cloves, crushed
2 fat red chillies, deseeded
    and finely chopped
1 tbsp ground cumin
400g/14oz canned
    chopped tomatoes
1.2 litres/2 pints boiling water
salt and freshly ground
    black pepper
Tabasco sauce (optional)

Rinse the black beans under cold running water. Drain and tip them into a large pan and cover with fresh cold water. Bring to the boil and boil rapidly for 10–12 minutes. Drain and rinse them and transfer them to the ceramic slow cooker pot.

Heat the oil in a large deep frying pan over a medium-high heat and fry the chicken for 4–5 minutes until browned on both sides.

Push the chicken to the side of the pan and add the onion and red pepper. Cook for 3–4 minutes, stirring occasionally, until they have softened slightly.

Add the garlic, chillies and cumin and cook, stirring constantly, for 1–2 minutes, until fragrant.

Add the tomatoes and boiling water and scrape up all the crispy bits from the bottom of the pan.

Carefully pour the mixture into the ceramic slow cooker pot, cover with the lid and cook on low for 10 hours. Check the chicken is cooked through and cook for longer if not.

FOR THE LIME AND
    CORIANDER CREAM
150ml/5½ fl oz crème fraiche
finely grated rind and
    juice of 1 unwaxed lime
chopped fresh coriander leaves
    and stems

crusty bread, to serve

Remove the chicken thighs from the soup. Use a stick blender to blend the soup for 10–20 seconds, to thicken it, but allow it to remain chunky.

Shred the chicken using two forks and discard the bones. Stir the chicken meat back into the soup. Season to taste. Add a dash of Tabasco sauce if you like your soup a little spicier.

To make the lime and coriander cream, mix together the crème fraiche, lime rind and juice and coriander.

Serve the soup drizzled with the lime and coriander cream, with hot crusty bread.

Cook's tip

Try using different cuts of meat in this soup: it works well using a ham hock. Cook as above and then remove the ham hock from the soup, checking it is cooked first. Cut away the rind, excess fat and bone from the ham hock. Shred the meat and stir it back into the soup. Watch out when seasoning this soup as the ham hock naturally contains a lot of salt, so you may only need to add pepper.

An easy peasy Mediterranean fish soup with rouille

With the abundance of fish available in the Mediterranean, it is no wonder fish soup is so popular.

PREP: 30 minutes
COOK: 4 hours
HEAT SETTING: high

SERVES 6

25g/1oz/2 tbsp butter
1 large onion, roughly chopped
4 rashers streaky bacon,
    roughly chopped
150ml/¼ pint dry white wine
600ml/1 pint hot fish stock
1 fresh bay leaf
1 fresh sprig tarragon
600g/1lb 5oz floury potatoes,
    finely diced
400g/14oz canned chopped
    tomatoes
2 tbsp tomato purée
450g/1lb fresh haddock
    fillets, skinned
150ml/¼ pint single cream
salt and freshly ground black pepper
8 thin slices French bread, toasted

FOR THE ROUILLE
1 large red pepper,
    roasted, skinned, deseeded
    and diced
1 garlic clove, roughly chopped
1 small fat red chilli, deseeded and
    roughly chopped
1 slice white bread, toasted

Heat the butter in a large frying pan over a medium heat and fry the onion and bacon for 3–4 minutes until the bacon is starting to crisp.

Pour in the white wine and let it bubble gently. Add the fish stock, bay leaf, tarragon, potatoes, tomatoes and tomato purée. Bring to the boil. Carefully pour the mixture into the ceramic slow cooker pot. Cover with the lid and cook on high for 3 hours.

Meanwhile, place the rouille ingredients in a food processor and process until smooth. Season to taste with salt and pepper. Chill the rouille, covered, until ready to use.

Cut the haddock into chunks and add to the soup. Cover and cook on high for 1 hour, then check the fish is cooked through.

Remove the tarragon sprig, then use a stick blender to purée the soup. Pass through a fine sieve and stir in the single cream.

Adjust the seasoning to taste. Ladle the soup into deep bowls.

Spread the toasted French bread with the rouille and serve 2 slices on each bowl of soup.

Warm smoked salmon and crab mousse

Do taste the mousse mixture as you go and add a little extra horseradish or lemon juice to suit your taste buds.

PREP: 20 minutes
COOK: 3 hours
HEAT SETTING: high
SERVES 4

300g/10½ oz sliced
    smoked salmon
200ml/7fl oz crème fraiche
4 egg yolks
finely grated rind and juice
    of 1 small unwaxed lemon
200g/7oz canned white
    crab meat, drained
1 tsp creamed horseradish
small handful chopped fresh
    flat-leaf parsley
salt and freshly ground
    black pepper

TO SERVE
shredded beetroot
lamb's lettuce and Swiss chard
Melba toast (optional)

Wet 4 x 150ml/¼ pint individual metal pudding basins and then line them with cling film, leaving some hanging over the rims (to cover the tops of the mousses later). Use the smoked salmon to line the base and sides of the pudding basins, again with enough overhanging the tops of the basins to cover the mousses later.

Whisk together the crème fraiche, egg yolks, lemon rind, 1 tablespoon of lemon juice, crab meat, horseradish and parsley. Season with salt and pepper. Spoon the mixture into the pudding basins and level the surface. Cover with the overhanging salmon and cling film.

Arrange the pudding basins in the base of the ceramic slow cooker pot and pour boiling water around them so that the water comes halfway up their sides. Cover with a lid and cook on high for 3 hours until the mousse is set.

Remove from the slow cooker and turn onto serving plates, discarding the cling film. Serve topped with beetroot, salad and Melba toast if wished.

Cook's tip

These little mousses can be served cold: simply remove from the slow cooker and leave at room temperature to cool, before chilling overnight in the fridge until firm.

Sweet pickled plums with blue cheese

It's difficult to understand until you have tasted these plums but they are great served with either sweet or savoury accompaniments: my favourite is a ripe creamy Dolcelatte or Gorgonzola cheese. Or try them with a rocket and walnut salad.

PREP: 10 minutes
COOK: 2½ hours
HEAT SETTING: high

MAKES 2 x 1.2 litre/2 pint
   KILNER JARS
700ml/1¼ pints cider vinegar
450g/1lb caster sugar
4 bay leaves
2 sprigs fresh rosemary
4 slices fresh root ginger,
   unpeeled
½ tsp salt
½ scant tsp black peppercorns
1kg/2lb 4oz firm red plums,
   washed
Dolcelatte, Gorgonzola or
   Stilton cheese, to serve

Pour the vinegar into the ceramic slow cooker pot. Stir in the sugar, bay leaves, rosemary, ginger, salt and peppercorns. Cover with the lid and cook on high for 2½ hours, stirring once during the cooking.

Meanwhile, prick the plums all over with a cocktail stick. Sterilise clean Kilner jars by heating them in an oven preheated to 100°C/200°F/Gas mark 1 for 30 minutes.

Pack the plums tightly into the sterilised jars. Ladle the warm vinegar mixture over the plums, tucking the bay leaves down the sides of the jars and making sure the plums are completely covered with the syrup. Close the jars with the rubber seals in place and allow to cool completely.

Store in a cool, dark cupboard for 4 weeks before using. The plums will keep for up to 2 months. Once opened, the plums will keep in the fridge for up to 1 week.

Serve the plums with slivers of Dolcelatte, Gorgonzola or Stilton cheese.

Cook's tip

Vary the flavour by adding your favourite herbs and spices: for a fragrant, sweeter syrup, add lavender or vanilla sugar to the vinegar, or for a more robust flavour add 1 star anise and 1 cinnamon stick.

Thai pumpkin soup

With Thai ingredients now readily available in supermarkets, authentic Thai dishes are easy to achieve. For convenience, use a ready-made Thai curry paste.

PREP: 15 minutes
COOK: 6 hours
HEAT SETTING: low

SERVES 4

1 tbsp olive oil
1 large onion, roughly chopped
1kg/2lb 4oz pumpkin or butternut
    squash, deseeded and cut into
    small chunks
5cm/2 inches fresh root
    ginger, grated
1 tbsp Thai red curry paste
1.2 litres/2 pints hot
    vegetable stock
salt and freshly ground
    black pepper
½ small red onion, trimmed and
    cut into thin wedges
1 ripe tomato, deseeded
    and chopped
handful fresh coriander leaves and
    stems, roughly torn
4 tbsp coconut cream

Heat the oil in a large saucepan over a medium heat and fry the onion and pumpkin for 4–5 minutes until just beginning to soften slightly. Add the ginger and curry paste and fry for 1–2 minutes.

Add the vegetable stock and stir, scraping up any crispy bits on the bottom of the pan. Carefully pour the mixture into the ceramic slow cooker pot. Cover with the lid. Cook on low for 6 hours until the pumpkin is just tender.

Use a stick blender to blend the soup until smooth. Season to taste.

Scatter with the red onion, tomato and coriander and drizzle with the coconut cream.

Cook's tip

Look out for minced ginger in a tube or jar, which can be added to homemade curry pastes, soups and stews. It keeps well in the fridge; for jarred ginger, simply pour a little vegetable or corn oil over the ginger's surface to form a good seal, and screw on the lid securely – this helps the paste to keep longer.

Goan potato, spinach and pea soup

A meal in a bowl — serve this soup with all your favourite Indian accompaniments: poppadoms, parathas, naans or just a sprinkling of fresh coriander.

PREP: 15 minutes
COOK: 4 hours
HEAT SETTING: high

SERVES 4

2 tbsp vegetable oil
2 tsp black mustard seeds
1 large onion, roughly chopped
1 fat green chilli, deseeded and
    finely chopped
5cm/2 inches fresh root ginger,
    peeled and finely grated
2 tbsp korma curry paste
½ tsp ground turmeric
850ml/1½ pints boiling water
900g/2lb waxy potatoes, peeled
    and cut into small chunks
400ml/14fl oz canned
    full-fat coconut milk
225g/8oz frozen peas
salt and freshly ground
    black pepper
225g/8oz baby leaf spinach

Heat the oil in a large frying pan, add the mustard seeds, cover with a lid and cook for 1 minute, shaking the pan, until the mustard seeds pop.

Add the onion, chilli, ginger, curry paste and turmeric and cook for a further 1–2 minutes, stirring continuously.

Pour over the boiling water and scrape up any crispy bits from the bottom of the pan. Pour the mixture into the slow cooker and add the potatoes and coconut milk. Cover with the lid and cook on high for 3 hours until the potatoes are tender.

Add the peas, cover with the lid and cook on high for 1 hour. Season to taste.

Stir in the spinach until it is just beginning to wilt, then serve.

Cook's tip

Don't be confused between black and brown mustard seeds — black mustard seeds are slightly harder to find, and they have a more intense flavour. If you cannot get hold of them, then use black onion seeds instead.

Red onion soup with goat's cheese croûtes

The gooey texture of the goat's cheese alongside the crisp, crusty French bread is quite wonderful in this rich soup.

PREP: 25 minutes
COOK: 4 hours
HEAT SETTING: high

SERVES 4

1 tbsp olive oil, plus extra for
    drizzling
25g/1oz/2 tbsp butter
1.25kg/2lb 12oz red onions, sliced
1 tsp caster sugar
2 tbsp brandy
1 tbsp plain flour
125ml/4fl oz dry white wine
1 litre/1¾ pints hot
    beef stock
1 tsp fresh thyme leaves, plus
    extra for garnishing
salt and freshly ground black
    pepper

FOR THE GOAT'S
    CHEESE CROÛTES
4 thick slices day-old French stick
1 fat garlic clove
85g/3oz creamy goat's cheese

Heat the oil and butter in a large deep frying pan over a medium heat and fry the onions for 8–10 minutes until they begin to soften. Sprinkle over the caster sugar and brandy and heat for 1–2 minutes, stirring constantly, to cook off the alcohol.

Sprinkle over the flour and gradually add the wine and stock, stirring constantly, until well combined. Sprinkle over the thyme. Carefully pour the mixture into the ceramic slow cooker pot. Cover with the lid and cook on high for 4 hours, stirring once during the cooking.

For the croûtes, preheat the grill to hot 10 minutes before the end of the cooking time. Toast the French bread on each side until golden and then rub one side of each croûte with the garlic. Divide the goat's cheese between the croutes and spread it on one side of each piece of toast.

Season the soup with salt and pepper and ladle it into soup bowls. Arrange the goat's cheese croûtes on the top. Scatter over the thyme and drizzle with a little olive oil just before serving.

Cook's tip

The smell of onions cooking is one we all love. However, don't be tempted to lift the lid and keep stirring the onions; you will lose valuable steam that helps the slow-cooking process.

Cheesy sharing fondue

Try your favourite dippers in rich melting cheese flavoured with wine, beer or kirsch. I particularly like freshly steamed asparagus spears and baby sweetcorn; if you want something even simpler, breadsticks and chicory leaves.

PREP: 10 minutes
COOK: 50 minutes
HEAT SETTING: high

SERVES 4

25g/1oz/2 tbsp softened butter
½ small onion, very finely
    chopped
1 small garlic clove, crushed
1 level tbsp cornflour
200ml/7fl oz dry white wine
200g/7oz Gruyère cheese,
    coarsely grated
200g/7oz Emmental cheese,
    coarsely grated
freshly grated nutmeg

TO SERVE
cherry tomatoes
chicory leaves
steamed asparagus spears
steamed baby sweetcorn

Grease the inside of the ceramic slow cooker pot with the butter. Add the onion and garlic and cover with the lid. Turn the slow cooker to high. Don't worry, this is the one exception to the rule of half-filling the ceramic pot.

Mix the cornflour in a small bowl with 3 tablespoons of the wine until you have a creamy paste. Blend in the remaining wine and pour into the slow cooker. Stir in both cheeses and a little nutmeg. Cover with the lid and cook on high for 50 minutes, whisking once during cooking.

Whisk the melted cheese well and pour it into a warm serving bowl. Place it on a large platter and surround it with the dippers and vegetable crudités. Eat immediately.

Cook's tip

If you like, scatter over a little crumbled blue cheese and very finely chopped celery before serving your fondue.

Eggs en cocotte with smoked salmon

If you don't serve these as a starter, serve them for breakfast with hot buttered toast. They are perfect with a cuppa!

PREP: 10 minutes
COOK: 30 minutes
HEAT SETTING: high

SERVES 4

1 tbsp softened butter
175g/6oz sliced smoked salmon
4 medium eggs
4 tbsp double cream
1 tsp creamed horseradish
freshly grated nutmeg
pepper
hot buttered toast, to serve

Pour 2.5cm/1 inch hot water into the ceramic slow cooker pot and turn the slow cooker to high.

Butter 4 x 175ml/6fl oz ramekins. Use the salmon to line the base and sides of the ramekins. Break an egg into each dish.

Lightly beat the cream and horseradish together and spoon over the eggs. Add a little nutmeg and season with pepper.

Cover the top of each ramekin with cling film and place them in the slow cooker pot, if necessary adding extra water to come halfway up the sides of the dishes. Cover with the lid and cook on high for 30 minutes until the whites are set and the egg yolks are still soft. Check and cook for a little while longer if you like firmer egg yolks.

Serve with hot buttered toast.

Cook's tip

For an alternative, line the ramekins with Parma ham instead of salmon and use pesto instead of horseradish. Omit the nutmeg.

Baked ricotta and olive pâté

For all cheese fiends out there, this is the pâté for you. True Parmesan is made using animal rennet, but veggie-friendly alternatives can be found.

PREP: 10 minutes, plus overnight chilling
COOK: 3 hours
HEAT SETTING: high

SERVES 4–6

olive oil, for greasing
250g/9oz ricotta cheese
55g/2oz Parmesan cheese, finely grated
1 egg white, lightly beaten
215g/7½ oz canned butter beans, drained and rinsed
125g/4½ oz fresh white breadcrumbs
salt and freshly ground pepper
150g/5½ oz lemon and mint marinated mixed olives
8 semi-dried sun-blush tomatoes
toasted slices of ciabatta or focaccia, to serve

Line the base of a 450g/1lb loaf tin with greaseproof paper. (Check that the tin will fit into the base of your slow cooker before you start. You could use any heatproof container with the same volume.) Lightly oil the paper and sides of the tin.

Place the ricotta and Parmesan, egg white and butter beans into a bowl and use a stick blender to blend until smooth.

Stir in the breadcrumbs and season with salt and pepper. Spoon into the prepared tin and level the surface with the back of a wet spoon. Wrap the loaf tin tightly with foil.

Put a metal cookie cutter or upturned saucer into the base of the ceramic slow cooker pot and place the loaf tin on top. Carefully pour boiling water around the tin until it comes halfway up the sides. Cover with the lid and cook on high for 3 hours until the pâté is set.

Remove from the slow cooker and cool completely, then chill overnight. Scatter with the olives and sun-blush tomatoes and serve with toasted ciabatta or focaccia.

Red lentil, pepper and goat's cheese terrine

If there is any of this terrine left over, it's wonderful spread on warm tortilla wraps, sprinkled with crispy salad leaves, rolled up and popped into a lunchbox.

PREP: 15 minutes, plus
    3 hours chilling
COOK: 5 hours
HEAT SETTING: high

SERVES 4–6

225g/8oz red lentils
1 small onion, finely chopped
450ml/16fl oz hot vegetable stock
2 tbsp sun-dried tomato paste
125g/4½ oz soft
    goat's cheese
3 eggs, lightly beaten
salt and freshly ground
    black pepper
1 red pepper, roasted,
    skinned, deseeded and
    roughly chopped
1 yellow pepper, roasted,
    skinned, deseeded and
    roughly chopped
fresh rocket
crisp crackers or Melba toast,
    to serve

Rinse the lentils under cold running water. Tip them into the ceramic slow cooker pot and add the onion, stock and sun-dried tomato paste. Cover with the lid and cook on high for 2 hours, stirring once during the cooking to prevent the lentils sticking.

Remove the lid – the lentils should have broken down and softened – and turn off the slow cooker. Allow the lentils to cool in the ceramic pot and continue to absorb any cooking liquid.

Tip the lentils into a bowl and add the goat's cheese and eggs. Beat until well combined. Season with salt and pepper.

Lightly oil an 850 ml/1½ pint loaf tin and line the base with greaseproof paper. (Check that the tin will fit into the base of your slow cooker before you start. You could use any heatproof serving dish with the same volume.) Spoon the lentil mixture into the loaf tin and level the surface. Cover the top with cling film.

Put a metal cookie cutter or upturned saucer into the base of the slow cooker pot and place the loaf tin on top. Carefully pour in enough boiling water to come halfway up the sides of the tin. Cover and cook on high for 3 hours.

Carefully remove the loaf tin from the slow cooker, discard the cling film and scatter over the peppers to cover. Cool completely and then chill for at least 3 hours.

Carefully turn the pâté out of the tin and then cut it into thick slices. Scatter with fresh rocket and serve with crisp crackers or Melba toast.

Bakes

Rich steak, mushroom and pickled walnut pudding

This is the ultimate comfort food for a cold winter's day, packed with a rich gravy, rump steak and tasty mushrooms.

PREP: 25 minutes
COOK: 6 hours
HEAT SETTING: high

SERVES 4–6

55g/2oz butter
1 tbsp olive oil
2 large onions, finely sliced
125g/4½ oz chestnut mushrooms, quartered
1 tbsp chopped fresh rosemary leaves
1 tbsp plain flour
150ml/¼ pint hot beef stock
2 tsp Dijon mustard
1 tbsp Worcestershire sauce
650g/1lb 7oz lean rump steak, thinly sliced
4 pickled walnuts, quartered
salt and freshly ground black pepper
300g/10½ oz self-raising flour
small handful fresh chopped flat-leaf parsley
150g/5½ oz shredded beef suet

Use half the butter to grease a 1.4 litre/2½ pint pudding basin. Heat the remaining butter and the oil in a large frying pan over a medium-high heat and fry the onions for 5 minutes, until they begin to soften. Stir in the mushrooms and rosemary and fry for a further 3–4 minutes. Sprinkle over the plain flour and pour over the stock. Remove from the heat and stir in the mustard, Worcestershire sauce, steak and pickled walnuts. Season with salt and pepper.

Mix together the self-raising flour, parsley, ½ teaspoon salt, beef suet and 200ml/7fl oz cold water to form a soft dough. Lightly flour a work surface and roll out the pastry, with a rolling pin, into a 34cm/13½ inch circle. Cut out a quarter segment and set aside. Lift up the remaining three-quarters of the circle and use it to line the base and sides of the greased pudding basin. Press the joined edges together to seal. Spoon in the filling.

Roll out the reserved quarter of pastry into a circle large enough to cover the top of the pudding basin. Dampen the edges and press them firmly together to seal and trim away any overhanging pastry. Cover the top with a piece of buttered greaseproof paper and then a piece of foil. Tie on a string handle.

Put an upturned saucer or metal cookie cutter into the bottom of the ceramic slow cooker pot. Stand the pudding basin on top and pour in enough boiling water to come halfway up the side of the pudding basin. Cover with the lid and cook on high for 6 hours until the beef is tender and cooked through.

Carefully remove the pudding basin and discard the wrappings. Turn the pudding out onto a warm serving plate.

Classic Greek moussaka

Serve this with a traditional Greek-style salad – roughly torn lettuce, chunky juicy tomato wedges, cucumber and lots of mint.

PREP: 35 minutes
COOK: 9 hours
HEAT SETTING: low

SERVES 4

3 tbsp olive oil
1 large aubergine, thinly sliced
500g/1lb 2oz minced lamb
1 large onion, finely chopped
2 tbsp plain flour
400g/14oz canned chopped
    tomatoes with garlic
2 tbsp tomato purée
200ml/7fl oz hot
    lamb stock
1 tsp ground cinnamon
1 tsp dried oregano
salt and freshly ground
    black pepper
3 medium eggs
225g/8oz natural yoghurt
85g/3oz feta cheese,
    finely crumbled
small handful fresh flat-leaf
    parsley, very finely chopped
55g/2oz fresh white
    breadcrumbs
grated nutmeg

Heat 1 tablespoon of the oil in a large frying pan over a medium-high heat and fry half the aubergine, until browned on both sides. Remove with a slotted spoon and set aside. Add another tablespoon of oil to the frying pan and fry the remaining aubergine. Remove and set aside.

Add the remaining oil to the frying pan and fry the minced lamb and onion for 6–8 minutes until browned, breaking up the lamb with a wooden spoon as it cooks.

Sprinkle over the flour and stir until well combined. Add the tomatoes, tomato purée, stock, cinnamon and oregano and simmer for 5–6 minutes. Season with a little salt and pepper and bring to the boil.

Transfer a couple of tablespoonfuls of the lamb mixture to the ceramic slow cooker pot. Arrange a layer of aubergine on top and then cover this with more of the lamb mixture. Repeat these layers, finishing with a layer of lamb. Cover with the lid and cook on low for 8 hours until the mince is tender and cooked through.

Meanwhile, in a bowl, mix the eggs, yoghurt, feta, parsley and breadcrumbs together. Spoon this mixture over the moussaka and sprinkle with a pinch of nutmeg. Cover with the lid and cook on low for 1 hour, until cooked through.

Preheat the grill to hot. Place the moussaka under the grill until the top is golden and bubbling.

Boston baked beans

I have made this dish on a few occasions and the beans have cooked differently each time. Taste as you go along; you may need to add a little boiling water and cook the bean mixture for another 30 minutes.

PREP: 20 minutes
COOK: 10–10½ hours
HEAT SETTING: low

SERVES 6

350g/12oz dried haricot beans,
    soaked overnight in
    cold water
225g/8oz salt belly pork,
    cut into small cubes
2 large Spanish onions,
    roughly chopped
1 large carrot, finely diced
2 celery sticks, strings removed
    and finely diced
2 tsp mustard powder
1 tsp salt
85g/3oz soft brown sugar
3 tbsp dark treacle
1 bay leaf
500ml/18fl oz passata
4 tbsp tomato purée

Rinse the beans under cold running water and place in a large saucepan. Cover with fresh cold water, bring to the boil and boil rapidly for 10 minutes. Drain and tip them into the ceramic slow cooker pot. (Alternatively, if time is short, use 2 x 300g/10½ oz cans haricot beans and just drain and rinse the beans.)

Add the pork, onions, carrot and celery.

Stir all the remaining ingredients together in a saucepan and heat until just before it boils. Pour over the bean mixture. Cover with the lid and cook on low for 10–10½ hours until the beans are tender and the pork is cooked through.

Mushroom, chestnut and veggie sausage pie

Rich and satisfying, this vegetarian pie will have you coming back for seconds. Vacuum-packed chestnuts add a great texture and flavour to this pie — they can usually be found next to all the ready-prepared stuffing mixes on the supermarket shelves.

PREP: 45 minutes
COOK: 6 hours
HEAT SETTING: low

SERVES 4

1 tbsp olive oil
1 large onion, roughly chopped
8 vegetarian Quorn sausages
    (not potato based), each
    cut into 3 pieces
2 large carrots, cut into chunks
450g/1lb chestnut mushrooms,
    halved
1 tbsp chopped fresh sage
2 tbsp plain flour
600ml/1 pint hot vegetable stock
1 tbsp wholegrain mustard
225g/8oz pack vacuum-packed
    chestnuts, crumbled
salt and freshly ground black
    pepper
1 large courgette, trimmed and
    cut into chunks
675g/1½ lb floury potatoes, cut
    into chunks
150g/5½ oz Savoy cabbage,
    shredded
25g/1oz/2 tbsp butter
3 tbsp crème fraiche
2 tsp creamed horseradish
400g/14oz canned green lentils,
    drained and rinsed

Heat the oil in a large frying pan over a medium heat and fry the onion and sausages for 5 minutes, until browned. Add the carrots and mushrooms and fry for 3–4 minutes, until the mushrooms are soft.

Sprinkle over the sage and flour, then stir until all the ingredients are coated with the flour. Gradually stir in the stock. Bring to the boil and simmer until thickened. Stir in the mustard and chestnuts and season with salt and pepper.

Tip the mixture into the ceramic slow cooker pot and stir in the courgette. Cover with the lid and cook on low for 6 hours.

Thirty minutes before the end of the cooking time, cook the potatoes in a large pan of lightly salted boiling water for 15–20 minutes until almost tender. Add the cabbage and cook for a further 5 minutes. Drain well and add half the butter, the crème fraîche and horseradish. Mash well with a fork.

Preheat the grill to hot. Stir the lentils into the vegetable mixture and then spoon the potatoes over the surface of the bake to cover it completely. Dot with the remaining butter and grill for 3–4 minutes, until golden.

Creamy potato, thyme and bacon bake

This is great as an accompaniment to chargrilled meats or as part of the Sunday roast dinner.

PREP: 20 minutes
COOK: 5½ hours
HEAT SETTING: high

SERVES 4

55g/2oz butter
1 large Spanish onion,
    thinly sliced
1 tsp dried thyme
175g/6oz smoked streaky bacon,
    roughly chopped
750g/1lb 10oz waxy potatoes,
    very thinly sliced
salt and freshly ground
    black pepper
425ml/¾ pint hot chicken stock
55g/2oz Gruyère cheese, grated
150ml/¼ pint double cream

Use all the butter to grease the ceramic slow cooker pot. Layer the onion, thyme and bacon with the potatoes in overlapping layers, seasoning with salt and pepper between each layer. Finish off with a layer of the onion, thyme and bacon.

Pour over the chicken stock. Cover with the lid and cook on high for 5 hours, until the potatoes are tender.

Sprinkle with the Gruyère and pour over the double cream. Cover with the lid and cook on high for 30 minutes.

Cook's tip

For a golden topping pop the bake under a preheated hot grill for 2–3 minutes until golden and bubbling.

Simple Mediterranean slow-roast lamb shanks

This lamb is so tender that it just falls off the bone. Serve with creamy mash or with plenty of crusty bread to mop up the juices.

PREP: 25 minutes
COOK: 6 hours
HEAT SETTING: high

SERVES 4

25g/1oz/2 tbsp butter
1 tbsp olive oil
4 x 350g/12oz lamb shanks
1 large red onion, cut into
    thin wedges
1 red pepper, deseeded, cored
    and cut into chunks
1 yellow pepper, deseeded, cored
    and cut into chunks
2 tbsp plain flour
200ml/7fl oz dry white wine
450ml/¾ pint hot lamb stock
400g/14oz canned cherry
    tomatoes
1 tbsp tomato purée
2 tbsp chopped fresh
    rosemary leaves
1 garlic bulb, halved horizontally
large handful chopped fresh
    flat-leaf parsley leaves
salt and freshly ground
    black pepper
mashed potato, to serve

Heat the butter and oil in a large frying pan over a medium-high heat and fry the lamb shanks, turning often, until well browned. Transfer with a slotted spoon to the ceramic slow cooker pot.

Add the onion to the pan and fry for 5 minutes, until it begins to soften. Add the peppers and cook for 2 minutes.

Sprinkle over the flour and gradually stir in the wine and stock, then bring to the boil, scraping up any crispy bits from the bottom of the pan. Add the cherry tomatoes, tomato purée, rosemary and garlic. Tip the mixture over the lamb shanks, pushing the garlic under the liquid. Cover with the lid and cook on high for 6 hours, or until the meat is falling off the bone.

Lift the garlic cloves out of the sauce and discard the papery skin, then mash the garlic cloves with a fork and stir them back into the sauce. Season to taste and scatter with parsley. Serve with mashed potato.

Greek lamb steaks with potatoes and minted yoghurt

The Greeks serve this dish with lots of bread, which they rub with garlic and then dip into the juices. These steaks make a gorgeous supper with some chargrilled courgette slices.

PREP: 25 minutes
COOK: 7 hours
HEAT SETTING: high

SERVES 4

2 tbsp plain flour
2 tsp dried oregano
4 lamb leg steaks
1 tbsp olive oil
2 large onions, sliced
3 fat garlic cloves, crushed
600ml/1 pint hot lamb stock
salt and freshly ground
    black pepper
2 large King Edward
    potatoes, sliced 5mm thick
4 beefsteak tomatoes,
    thickly sliced
150ml/¼ pint natural yoghurt,
    to serve
3 tbsp mint sauce, to serve

Combine the flour and oregano on a plate and toss the lamb steaks in the mixture. Heat the oil in a large frying pan over a medium-high heat and fry the lamb on each side for 2 minutes until browned. Remove to a warm plate using a slotted spoon.

Add the onions to the frying pan and fry for 5 minutes, until they begin to soften. Stir in the garlic and cook for a further 2 minutes. Sprinkle over any leftover flour mixture and gradually stir in the stock. Season with salt and pepper.

Layer the lamb steaks, potatoes, sauce and tomatoes in the ceramic slow cooker pot. Repeat, finishing with a layer of tomatoes. Cover with the lid and cook on high for 7 hours or until the potatoes and lamb are tender and cooked through.

Mix together the yoghurt and mint sauce and season to taste. Serve with the lamb steaks and potatoes and chargrilled courgette slices, if you wish.

Lamb with pomegranate and honey

Pomegranates are readily available in most large supermarkets and greengrocers. Simply roll the pomegranate on a work surface, pressing down slightly to loosen the seeds, then cut it open and use a teaspoon to scrape the seeds away from the white membrane.

PREP: 20 minutes
COOK: 7 hours
HEAT SETTING: high

SERVES 4

1 tbsp olive oil
1kg/2lb 4oz half shoulder
    of lamb
3 fat garlic cloves,
    roughly chopped
2.5cm/1 inch fresh root ginger,
    finely chopped
2 tbsp plain flour
450ml/16fl oz hot
    lamb stock
1 tsp ground cinnamon
large pinch saffron threads
175g/6oz frozen button onions
3 tbsp runny honey
salt and freshly ground
    black pepper
seeds from 1 pomegranate
fresh small mint leaves

Heat the oil in a large frying pan over a medium–high heat and fry the lamb on each side until well browned. Carefully transfer with 2 slotted spoons to the ceramic slow cooker pot.

Add the garlic and ginger to the frying pan and cook for 1 minute.

Sprinkle over the flour and gradually stir in the stock, cinnamon and saffron, scraping up any crispy bits on the bottom of the pan. Bring to the boil, then stir in the onions and pour the mixture over the lamb. Cover with the lid and cook on high for 7 hours until the meat is tender and falling off the bone. (You should be able to insert a fork into the meat and it will fall off the bone very easily.)

Stir in the honey and season with salt and pepper. Scatter with the pomegranate seeds and mint leaves.

Gamekeeper's pie

I have given this pie a traditional topping of puff pastry, which does mean using your oven.

PREP: 25 minutes, plus 25–30
    minutes in an oven
COOK: 8 hours
HEAT SETTING: low

SERVES 4

25g/1oz/2 tbsp butter
1 tbsp olive oil
750g/1lb 10oz venison, cut into
    2.5cm/1 inch dice
2 red onions, cut into thin wedges
2 celery sticks, strings
    removed and sliced
2 carrots, diced
6 rashers rindless streaky bacon,
    sliced
150g/5½ oz baby button
    mushrooms
2 tsp minced garlic
2 tbsp plain flour
Maldon sea salt and freshly
    ground black pepper
225ml/8fl oz full-bodied
    red wine
300ml/½ pint hot beef stock
1 tbsp tomato purée
2 tbsp redcurrant jelly
large handful chopped fresh
    flat-leaf parsley
350g/12oz ready-made puff pastry
1 egg, lightly beaten
fresh thyme leaves

Heat the butter and oil in a large shallow frying pan over a medium-high heat and fry the venison, in batches if necessary, until well browned. Transfer with a slotted spoon to the ceramic slow cooker pot.

Add the onions, celery, carrots, bacon and mushrooms to the frying pan and fry for 5 minutes until soft. Stir in the garlic and cook for 1 minute.

Sprinkle over the flour and 1 teaspoon of pepper, then gradually stir in the wine, stock, tomato purée, redcurrant jelly and parsley. Bring to the boil, scraping up any crispy bits on the base of the pan, and then pour the mixture over the venison. Cover with the lid and cook on low for 8 hours until the meat is meltingly tender and cooked through. Season to taste.

Preheat the oven to 200°C/400°F/Gas mark 6. Roll out the puff pastry using a rolling pin, on a lightly floured surface so that it is large enough to cover the top of your pie dish with about 2.5cm/1 inch extra all the way around. Lay the top of the pie dish onto the pastry and cut around the edge. Then cut a strip about 2.5cm/1 inch wide all the way around the pie lid, leaving the pie dish in place to guide you.

Spoon the casserole mixture into the pie dish. Brush the rim of the dish with water and line with the 2.5cm/1 inch pastry strip. Brush the pastry rim with beaten egg and lay the pastry lid on top to cover the filling completely. Press the edges together to seal tightly.

Lightly score the pastry with a sharp knife in a criss-cross pattern. Make a slit in the centre of the lid to allow steam to escape, then brush with beaten egg and scatter with freshly ground black pepper, Maldon sea salt and thyme leaves. Bake in the preheated oven for 25–30 minutes until golden.

Chicken, bacon and apple sauce pie

Chicken thighs have so much flavour and, cooked in this way, with the sweet apple sauce and salty bacon, they become tender and moist. Stir in a handful of peas with the apple sauce, if you like. The fluffy cheesy scone topping can be brushed with a little melted butter and browned under a hot grill, too.

PREP: 25 minutes
COOK: 8 hours
HEAT SETTING: low and high

SERVES 4

70g/2½ oz butter
1 tbsp vegetable oil
8 large skinless chicken thighs
6 rashers streaky bacon, sliced
1 large onion, roughly chopped
2 tbsp plain flour
600ml/1 pint hot chicken stock
225g/8oz self-raising flour
125g/4½ oz Cheddar cheese,
    finely grated
small handful snipped chives
1 medium egg, lightly beaten
5 tbsp full-fat milk
4 heaped tbsp apple sauce
salt and freshly ground
    black pepper
fine green beans, trimmed
    and blanched, to serve

Melt 25g/1oz/2 tbsp butter with the oil in a large frying pan over a medium-high heat and add the chicken and bacon. Fry for 4–5 minutes until browned. Transfer to the ceramic slow cooker pot with a slotted spoon.

Add the onion to the frying pan and fry for 5 minutes until it begins to soften. Sprinkle over the plain flour and gradually stir in the stock. Bring to the boil and simmer until thickened. Pour into the ceramic slow cooker pot. Cover with the lid and cook on low for 7 hours until the chicken is tender and cooked through.

After 6¾ hours, rub the remaining butter into the self-raising flour and stir in two-thirds of the Cheddar, the chives, egg and milk to form a firm dough. Roll out on a lightly floured surface to the same size as the base of your slow cooker pot. Cut into 8 triangles.

Stir the apple sauce into the chicken mixture and season to taste. Arrange the triangles over the top. Cover and cook on high for 1 hour.

Preheat the grill to hot. Sprinkle the remaining cheese over the scone topping and grill until melted and golden. Serve with blanched green beans.

Orange, ginger and coriander-soused salmon

Delicately poached salmon with spicy overtones, which is great served either warm or cold, with a crisp green salad.

PREP: 10 minutes
COOK: 2 hours
HEAT SETTING: low

SERVES 4

4 x 175g/6oz salmon fillets,
    skinned
salt and freshly ground black
    pepper
1 tbsp coriander seeds
150ml/¼ pint orange juice, freshly
    squeezed
finely grated rind and
    juice of 1 orange
2.5cm/1 inch fresh root ginger,
    peeled and finely grated
6 spring onions, trimmed, halved
    lengthways and shredded
3 fat garlic cloves, thinly sliced
2 fat red chillies, deseeded
    and sliced
3 tbsp dry white wine
squeeze of lemon juice (optional)
small handful fresh coriander
    leaves and stems
orange wedges (optional)

Make a double thickness strip of foil big enough to fit across the widest part of your ceramic slow cooker pot and up and over the side, so you can lift out the salmon easily. Lay the salmon on top and season with salt and pepper.

In a frying pan dry fry the coriander seeds until fragrant. Tip them into a pestle and mortar and crush to a powder. Sieve to remove any tough bits of the seeds.

Heat the orange juice in a small saucepan with the orange rind, ginger, spring onions, garlic, chillies and wine until it is hot but not boiling.

Stir in the coriander powder and pour the mixture over the salmon. Tuck the overhanging foil into the ceramic pot so that you can fit the lid on. Cover with the lid and cook on low for 2 hours or until the fish easily flakes with a fork. Lift the salmon out with the help of the foil.

Season the juices to taste and add a squeeze of fresh lemon juice, if necessary. Drizzle a few spoonfuls of the juices over the fish and scatter with the fresh coriander and orange wedges (if using).

Fish pie with saffron mash

Choose your favourite combination of fish for this pie: I often mix fresh and smoked haddock. Adding saffron threads to the potatoes' cooking water gives the mash a wonderful golden yellow colour.

PREP: 35 minutes
COOK: 1½–2 hours
HEAT SETTING: high

SERVES 4

450g/1lb fresh haddock
    fillets, skinned
85g/3oz butter
1 large leek, trimmed and
    thinly sliced
2 tbsp plain flour
300ml/½ pint full-fat milk
125g/4½ oz full-fat cream cheese
salt and pepper
125g/4½ oz cooked peeled
    cold-water prawns
1 tbsp chopped fresh dill or
    tarragon
675g/1½ lb potatoes, cut into
    chunks
large pinch saffron threads
3 tbsp crème fraiche
steamed broccoli, to serve

Cut the fish into bite-sized pieces and set aside.

Melt half the butter in a large frying pan and sauté the leek for 5 minutes, until it just begins to soften. Sprinkle over the plain flour and cook, stirring constantly, for 1 minute. Gradually stir in the milk and cream cheese and simmer until smooth and thick.

Remove from the heat and season with salt and pepper. Stir in the fish, prawns and dill. Spoon the mixture into the ceramic slow cooker pot. Cover with the lid and cook on high for 1½–2 hours until the fish is white and flakes easily.

Thirty minutes before the end of the cooking time, cook the potatoes and saffron in a large pan of lightly salted boiling water for 15–20 minutes, until tender. Drain well and add the remaining butter and crème fraiche. Mash until smooth.

Preheat the grill to hot. Spoon the saffron mash over the fish sauce to cover it completely and grill for 2–3 minutes until golden. Serve with steamed broccoli.

Tomato, spinach and goat's cheese cannelloni

This is a great mid-week supper dish. It doesn't really matter what type of tomato pasta sauce you use, so just choose your favourite.

PREP: 20 minutes
COOK: 1–1½ hours
HEAT SETTING: high

SERVES 4

225g/8oz baby leaf spinach
250g/9oz soft goat's cheese
salt and freshly ground
    black pepper
freshly grated nutmeg
8 fresh lasagne sheets
560g/1lb 4½ oz tomato
    pasta sauce
55g/2oz mozzarella cheese,
    grated
dressed salad leaves, to serve

Rinse the spinach under cold running water and drain. Put into a saucepan with no extra water and heat gently, stirring occasionally, until it wilts. Drain well.

Tip the spinach into a bowl and stir in the goat's cheese. Season with salt, pepper and nutmeg. Spread the mixture thinly all over the lasagne sheets. Roll up the sheets tightly from the short end.

Pour half the tomato sauce into the base of the ceramic slow cooker pot. Arrange the cannelloni over the sauce, in a single layer if possible. Pour over the remaining sauce. Cover and cook on high for 1–1½ hours.

Sprinkle over the mozzarella cheese and serve with salad leaves.

Gruyère and mustard bread pudding

Everyone likes bread-and-butter pudding, but rather than making the traditional sweet version, why not surprise your friends and family with this savoury dish — it's just as moreish. Serve with crispy bacon or sausages and Tomato and Chilli Jam (see page 244).

PREP: 25 minutes, plus
    30 minutes soaking
COOK: 4 hours
HEAT SETTING: low

SERVES 4

85g/3oz softened butter
2 tsp wholegrain mustard
½ French stick, thickly sliced
300ml/½ pint full-fat milk
3 medium eggs
4 tbsp freshly grated
    Parmesan cheese
large pinch cayenne pepper
125g/4½ oz Gruyère
    cheese, grated

Use 25g/1oz butter to grease a 1.2 litre/2 pint heatproof dish that will easily fit into the base of your ceramic slow cooker pot.

Mix together the remaining butter and the mustard and spread it on one side of the sliced bread. Arrange the bread in a single overlapping layer in the heatproof dish, mustard side up.

Whisk the milk, eggs, half the Parmesan cheese, the cayenne and Gruyère together and pour over the bread. Push the bread into the liquid and set aside to soak for 30 minutes.

Sprinkle over the remaining Parmesan. Cover tightly with foil. Put an upturned saucer or metal cookie cutter into the base of the slow cooker pot and lower the heatproof dish onto the saucer or metal cookie cutter (using a wide folded strip of foil to make it easier to lift the hot dish out). Cover with the lid and cook on low for 4 hours.

Preheat the grill to hot. Place the heatproof dish under the grill for 2–3 minutes, until the top is golden.

Stews, casseroles & sauces

Classic beef hotpot

**A classic recipe that I have adapted for the slow cooker –
why change something that's already so delicious?**

PREP: 25 minutes
COOK: 8 hours
HEAT SETTING: high

SERVES 4

2 tbsp olive oil
750g/1lb 10oz braising
    steak, cubed
3 celery sticks (strings
    removed), sliced
2 onions, roughly chopped
2 tbsp plain flour
600ml/1 pint hot beef stock
1 tbsp Worcestershire sauce
1 tbsp wholegrain mustard
1 tbsp tomato purée
3 tbsp fresh thyme leaves
salt and freshly ground
    black pepper
2 large carrots, cut into chunks
2 large parsnips, cored and
    cut into chunks
2 large baking potatoes,
    thinly sliced
steamed and buttered Savoy
    cabbage, to serve

Heat 1 tablespoon of the oil in a large frying pan over a medium-high heat and fry the beef, in batches if necessary, for 4–5 minutes until well browned. Transfer it to the ceramic slow cooker pot with a slotted spoon.

Add the remaining oil to the frying pan and fry the celery and onions for 5 minutes until the onion begins to soften. Sprinkle over the flour and then gradually stir in the stock followed by the Worcestershire sauce, wholegrain mustard, tomato purée and thyme leaves. Bring to the boil and season with salt and pepper.

Scatter the carrots and parsnips over the meat and pour over just enough gravy to cover.

Arrange the potatoes in overlapping layers to cover the meat and vegetables, then place a layer of buttered greaseproof paper on top and push down slightly so that the potatoes are pushed into the gravy. Cover with the lid and cook on high for 8 hours until the meat and potatoes are tender and cooked through.

Serve with steamed and buttered Savoy cabbage.

Louisiana beef chilli

They don't do things by halves in Louisiana, as you can tell from this chunky beefsteak chilli. If you don't like your chilli hot, use a mild chilli powder instead.

PREP: 20 minutes
COOK: 10 hours
HEAT SETTING: low

SERVES 4

1 tbsp olive oil
750g/1lb 10oz braising
    steak, cubed
1 large onion, cut into wedges
2 fat garlic cloves, crushed
2 tsp hot chilli powder
3 tbsp plain flour
300ml/½ pint hot beef stock
2 tbsp tomato purée
400g/14oz canned chopped
    tomatoes with peppers
    and chilli
800g/1lb 12oz canned red kidney
    beans, drained and rinsed
2 large red peppers,
    cored, deseeded and cut
    into chunks
salt and freshly ground
    black pepper
small handful chopped fresh
    coriander

TO SERVE
tortilla chips
guacamole
steamed long grain rice (optional)

Heat the oil in a large frying pan over a medium-high heat and fry the beef, in batches if necessary, until well browned all over. Transfer it to the ceramic slow cooker pot with a slotted spoon.

Add the onion to the frying pan and fry for 4–5 minutes, stirring occasionally, until soft and beginning to brown. Stir in the garlic and chilli powder and cook for 1 minute more.

Sprinkle over the flour and then gradually stir in the stock followed by the tomato purée and tomatoes. Bring to the boil, scraping up any crispy bits on the bottom of the pan. Transfer the mixture to the ceramic slow cooker pot and stir well. Add the kidney beans and red peppers. Cover with the lid and cook on low for 10 hours until the meat is tender and cooked through.

Season with salt and pepper and scatter with coriander. Serve with tortilla chips and guacamole, and long grain rice if you wish.

Country beef, beer and barley casserole

I grew up eating pearl barley in soups and stews — it's a very Scottish thing. I love it and that's why in this wonderful rich meat stew I use pearl barley instead of serving the dish with potatoes. Just spoon it into a bowl and eat with hot crusty bread.

PREP: 25 minutes
COOK: 8½–9 hours
HEAT SETTING: low

SERVES 4

2 tbsp olive oil
650g/1lb 7oz stewing steak,
    cubed
1 large onion, cut into large
    chunks
1 tbsp plain flour
300ml/½ pint beer
700ml/1¼ pints hot beef stock
2 tbsp fresh thyme leaves
salt and freshly ground black
    pepper
300g/10½ oz Chantenay carrots
300g/10½ oz swede, cut
    into small chunks
125g/4½ oz pearl barley
small handful chopped
    fresh flat-leaf parsley

Heat 1 tablespoon of oil in a large shallow frying pan over a medium-high heat and fry the beef, in batches if necessary, for 4–5 minutes until well browned. Transfer the cooked beef to the ceramic slow cooker pot using a slotted spoon.

Add the remaining oil to the frying pan and fry the onion for 5–6 minutes until it begins to soften. Sprinkle over the flour and then gradually stir in the beer and stock and bring to the boil. Stir in the thyme and season with salt and pepper.

Pour the mixture over the beef and scatter over the carrots, swede and pearl barley. Cover with the lid and cook on low for 8½–9 hours until the beef is tender and cooked through. Stir in the parsley before serving.

White bean and rosemary stew with Brie crust

If you love breaking into a baked Camembert to reveal the oozing cheese inside, then you will love this dish too, as you break through the cheese crust to reveal little jewel-like vegetables simmered in a rich tomato sauce. You can use cannellini or haricot beans for this recipe.

PREP: 20 minutes
COOK: 4 hours
Heat setting: high

SERVES 4

2 tbsp olive oil
1 large red onion, roughly
    chopped
1 small aubergine, trimmed and
    cut into chunks
1 large red pepper, cored,
    deseeded and cut into chunks
1 orange pepper, cored,
    deseeded and cut into chunks
1 large courgette, trimmed and
    cut into chunks
2 fat garlic cloves, crushed
1 tbsp plain flour
400g/14oz canned cherry
    tomatoes
150ml/¼ pint hot
    vegetable stock
2 tbsp chopped fresh
    rosemary leaves
800g/1lb 12oz canned cannellini
    beans, drained and rinsed
salt and freshly ground pepper
1 mini whole Brie
    (about 225g/8oz)

Heat the oil in a large deep frying pan over a medium heat and fry the onion, aubergine and peppers for 5 minutes, stirring occasionally, until they have softened slightly. Add the courgette and garlic and cook for 2 minutes.

Sprinkle over the flour and stir well until all the vegetables are coated. Add the cherry tomatoes, stock and rosemary and bring to the boil. Transfer the mixture into the ceramic slow cooker pot. Cover with the lid and cook on high for 3½ hours until the vegetables are tender.

Stir in the beans. Cover with the lid and cook on high for a further 30 minutes. Season with salt and pepper.

Preheat the grill to hot. Slice the Brie as thinly as you can and arrange over the vegetables so they are covered. Place the ceramic slow cooker pot under the grill for 2–3 minutes until the cheese is bubbling and golden.

Hearty venison and red cabbage stew

If you think red cabbage can only be used for coleslaw, then think again. It is the ideal vegetable to cook alongside rich venison. Venison is becoming more readily available in supermarkets now. If you cannot find diced venison, simply buy the steaks and cut them into chunks.

PREP: 25 minutes
COOK: 10 hours
HEAT SETTING: low

SERVES 4

1 tbsp olive oil
750g/1lb 10oz venison, cubed
25g/1oz/2 tbsp butter
¼ small red cabbage, cored and
    finely shredded
225g/8oz frozen pearl onions
2 fat garlic cloves, crushed
2 tbsp plain flour
200ml/7fl oz red wine
225ml/8fl oz hot beef stock
1 tbsp tomato purée
3 tbsp cranberry sauce
125g/4½ oz dried cranberries
2 tbsp fresh thyme leaves
salt and freshly ground black
    pepper

TO SERVE
mashed potato
green beans

Heat the oil in a large shallow frying pan over a medium-high heat and fry the venison, in batches if necessary, for 4–5 minutes until well browned. Transfer the mixture to the ceramic slow cooker pot with a slotted spoon.

Add the butter to the frying pan and fry the red cabbage for 6–8 minutes, stirring regularly. Tip the cabbage over the venison and add the pearl onions and stir well.

Add the garlic to the frying pan and fry for 1 minute. Sprinkle over the flour and then gradually stir in the wine, stock, tomato purée, cranberry sauce, cranberries and thyme leaves. Bring to the boil, scraping up any crispy bits on the bottom of the pan.

Pour the gravy over the venison mixture. Cover with the lid and cook on low for 10 hours until the meat is meltingly tender and cooked through. Season with salt and pepper and serve with buttery mashed potatoes and green beans.

Italian beef, ricotta and spinach meatballs

Meatballs and spaghetti — just like Mamma used to make — you can't beat it. Sprinkle over a little freshly grated Parmesan cheese and you might even think you were on holiday in Italy.

PREP: 30 minutes
COOK: 6 hours
HEAT SETTING: high

SERVES 4

FOR THE MEATBALLS
2 tbsp olive oil
1 small onion, finely chopped
1 fat garlic clove
2 tbsp fresh thyme leaves
175g/6oz baby leaf spinach
2 tbsp ricotta cheese
1 medium egg yolk
finely grated rind of
    1 unwaxed lemon
450g/1lb extra-lean minced beef
salt and freshly ground black
    pepper

FOR THE SAUCE
1 tbsp olive oil
1 red onion, roughly chopped
2 fat garlic cloves, crushed
400g/14oz canned
    chopped tomatoes
2 tsp caster sugar
150ml/¼ pint hot chicken stock

TO SERVE
cooked spaghetti
fresh basil leaves
finely grated Parmesan cheese

To make the meatballs, heat half the oil in a large frying pan over a medium heat and fry the onion, garlic and thyme for 2–3 minutes until softened.

Stir in the spinach and cook for 1 minute until wilted. Tip the spinach mixture into a food processor and add the ricotta, egg yolk, lemon rind, minced beef and salt and pepper. Process until finely chopped and well combined.

Roll the minced beef mixture into 20 walnut-sized balls. Heat the remaining oil (for the meatballs) in a large frying pan and fry the meatballs, in batches if necessary, until browned. Transfer them to the ceramic slow cooker pot with a slotted spoon.

To make the sauce, heat the oil in the frying pan over a medium heat and fry the onion for 5 minutes until it has softened slightly. Add the garlic and cook for a further 1–2 minutes.

Stir in the tomatoes, sugar and stock and bring to the boil. Pour this mixture over the meatballs. Cover with the lid and cook on high for 6 hours until the meatballs are cooked through.

Serve with spaghetti, fresh basil and finely grated Parmesan.

Bistro-style Bolognese

The long slow-cooking process really boosts the flavour of this Bolognese. I normally keep a batch or two of this sauce in the freezer so I can take out a portion before I go to work and reheat it when I come home – it's great to have dinner on the table in the time it takes to cook a pan of pasta!

PREP: 20 minutes
COOK: 10 hours
HEAT SETTING: low

SERVES 4

55g/2oz dried wild
    mixed mushrooms
150ml/¼ pint hot beef stock
1 tbsp olive oil
450g/1lb lean minced beef
1 large red onion, finely chopped
225g/8oz chicken livers, trimmed
    and roughly chopped
2 tsp minced garlic
6 rashers smoked streaky bacon,
    roughly chopped
2 tbsp fresh thyme leaves
1 tbsp plain flour
150ml/¼ pint full-bodied
    red wine
400g/14oz canned cherry
    tomatoes
2 tbsp sun-dried tomato paste
salt and freshly ground black
    pepper

TO SERVE
cooked penne pasta
Parmesan cheese, freshly grated
fresh basil

Stir the wild mushrooms into the hot stock and leave to soak for at least 15 minutes.

Meanwhile, heat the olive oil in a large frying pan over a medium-high heat and fry the minced beef, onion, chicken livers, garlic and bacon for 8–10 minutes, stirring occasionally, until browned. Sprinkle over the thyme and flour and stir, then cook for 1–2 minutes more.

Transfer the mixture to the ceramic slow cooker pot. Stir in the wine, tomatoes, sun-dried tomato paste, wild mushrooms and stock. Cover with the lid and cook on low for 10 hours until the meat is tender and cooked through.

Stir well and season with salt and pepper. Serve with the pasta and scatter with freshly grated Parmesan cheese and basil.

Lamb cobbler

I love to see the suspense on my family's and friends' faces when I make this recipe. What will be beneath the crisp buttery scone top? A delicious meaty minced lamb gravy — it's all about comfort, comfort, comfort.

PREP: 30 minutes
COOK: 8 hours
HEAT SETTING: low and high

SERVES 4

3 tbsp olive oil
450g/1lb lean minced lamb
1 onion, finely chopped
2 carrots, finely diced
2 fat garlic cloves, crushed
1 tbsp plain flour
400g/14oz canned
    chopped tomatoes
200ml/7fl oz hot lamb stock
1 tsp ground cinnamon
1 tbsp tomato purée
salt and freshly ground
    black pepper
175g/6oz frozen peas

For the cobbler topping
200g/7oz self-raising flour
55g/2oz butter
85g/3oz mature Cheddar
    cheese, grated
1 medium egg, beaten
5 tbsp full-fat milk

Heat the oil in a large frying pan and fry the minced lamb, onion, carrots and garlic for 8–10 minutes, stirring occasionally, until well browned.

Sprinkle over the flour and then stir in the chopped tomatoes, stock, cinnamon and tomato purée. Bring to the boil and season with salt and pepper. Transfer the mixture to the ceramic slow cooker pot. Cover with the lid and cook on low for 7 hours until the lamb is tender and cooked through.

To make the cobbler topping, sift the flour into a large bowl and rub in the butter. Stir in the Cheddar, egg and 4 tablespoons of the milk to form a soft, pliable dough.

Roll out the dough on a lightly floured surface to about 2cm/¾ inch thick. Use a 6cm/2½ inch plain cookie cutter to stamp out 8 scones.

Brush the top of the scones with the remaining milk. Stir the peas into the minced lamb mixture. Arrange the scones over the top of the lamb. Cover with the lid and cook on high for 45 minutes. If you like, place the ceramic slow cooker pot under a hot grill to brown the scones.

Pork chops with cider gravy and herby dumplings

When was the last time you had dumplings? It's high time to rediscover them as they are comforting and, with this dish of tender pork chops and rich cider gravy, you're on to a winter warming winner!

PREP: 20 minutes
COOK: 6 hours
HEAT SETTING: low

SERVES 4

1 tbsp olive oil
25g/1oz/2 tbsp butter
1 large onion, cut into chunks
175g/6oz chestnut
    mushrooms, quartered
4 x large pork loin chops
175g/6oz plain flour
salt and freshly ground black
    pepper
finely grated rind and
    juice of 1 unwaxed lemon
300ml/½ pint dry cider
300ml/½ pint hot chicken stock
1 tbsp wholegrain mustard
2 red-skinned dessert
    apples, cored and cut
    into thick wedges
1 large leek, thickly sliced
85g/3oz vegetable suet
small handful chopped fresh
    mixed herbs: parsley, chives,
    sage, rosemary leaves

Heat the oil and butter in a large frying pan over a medium heat and fry the onion and mushrooms for 5 minutes, until the onion begins to soften. Arrange the pork chops on a plate and scatter over 25g/1oz flour to coat them. Season with salt and pepper.

Tip the onion and mushrooms into the ceramic slow cooker pot. Add the pork chops to the frying pan and cook for a couple of minutes on each side to colour slightly. Lay the chops on the onion mixture.

Tip any excess flour from the pork chops' plate into the frying pan and add the lemon juice. Stir in the cider, stock and mustard and bring to the boil, scraping up any crispy bits from the bottom of the pan.

Tip the mixture into the ceramic slow cooker pot and scatter over the apples and leek. Cover with the lid and cook on low for 5 hours until the meat is tender and cooked through.

If you think the sauce needs thickening, simply add some cornflour, mixed to a smooth paste with cold water.

Meanwhile, to make the dumplings, mix together, in a large bowl, the remaining plain flour, the lemon rind, vegetable suet, herbs and 6 tablespoons of cold water. Bring the mixture together to form a soft pliable dough.

On a lightly floured surface pat the dough into a circle about 15cm/6 inches wide and cut into 8 triangles. Place over the pork chops, cover and cook on low for 1 hour until the dumplings have risen and are tender.

Spanish white bean, chorizo and potato stew

A hearty stew with a variety of flavours in every mouthful. I like to use a spicy chorizo sausage for a richer, fuller taste.

PREP: 15 minutes
COOK: 7 hours
HEAT SETTING: high

SERVES 4

1 tbsp olive oil
1 large onion, trimmed and cut
　　into wedges
450g/1lb dry-cured chorizo
　　sausage, thickly sliced
3 fat garlic cloves, crushed
1 tsp hot chilli powder
1/2 tsp smoked paprika
1 large red pepper, cored,
　　deseeded and cut into chunks
800g/1lb 12oz canned chopped
　　tomatoes
400g/14oz canned cannellini
　　beans, drained and rinsed
2 tbsp tomato purée
450g/1lb baby new potatoes,
　　halved
150g/5½ oz fine green
　　beans, trimmed
handful chopped fresh
　　flat-leaf parsley
crusty bread, to serve

Heat the oil in a large frying pan over a medium heat and fry the onion and chorizo for a few minutes until the chorizo oozes its red oil.

Stir in the garlic, chilli powder and paprika and cook for 1 minute, stirring continuously, until fragrant. Remove from the heat and pour over 5 tablespoons of boiling water. Stir, scraping up any crispy bits from the bottom of the pan. Tip into the ceramic slow cooker pot.

Add the red pepper to the pot, along with the chopped tomatoes, cannellini beans, tomato purée, potatoes and green beans. Stir well to combine, cover with the lid and cook on high for 7 hours.

Scatter over the flat-leaf parsley and serve with plenty of crusty bread to mop up the juices.

Pot-roast pheasant with prunes and bacon

Pheasant is a lean gamey meat, which is not just for special occasions. The light, tender white meat with the salty bacon and sweet prunes is a great combination.

PREP: 25 minutes
COOK: 4 hours
HEAT SETTING: high

SERVES 4

1 tbsp olive oil
25g/1oz/2 tbsp butter
1 pheasant
    (about 750g/1lb 10oz)
1 large onion, cut into wedges
85g/3oz streaky bacon,
    roughly chopped
1 tbsp plain flour
300ml/½ pint hot chicken stock
finely grated rind and juice of
    1 orange
175g/6oz ready-to-eat prunes,
    stones removed
3 tbsp sweet sherry
1 tbsp fresh thyme leaves
salt and freshly ground
    black pepper
fine green beans, trimmed and
    blanched, to serve

Heat the oil and butter in a large shallow frying pan over a medium-high heat and fry the pheasant all over for about 10 minutes until golden. Transfer to the ceramic slow cooker pot using 2 forks or slotted spoons.

Add the onion and bacon to the frying pan and fry for 5 minutes until the onion begins to soften and the bacon is crispy. Sprinkle over the flour and gradually stir in the chicken stock and orange rind and juice, followed by the prunes, sherry and thyme. Season with salt and pepper and bring to the boil.

Pour the gravy over the pheasant. Cover with the lid and cook on high for 3½ hours until the pheasant is cooked through. Test the thickest part of the thigh by piercing it with a skewer — if the juices run clear the bird is cooked; if they are slightly pink cover with the lid and cook on high for a further 30 minutes before testing again.

Serve with blanched green beans.

Gremolata braised chicken

Gremolata is a fresh, zesty garnish traditionally served with Osso Buco Milanese. Here it is used to add extra flavour to a rich, spicy chicken stew. Serve this with steamed couscous or creamy mashed potato.

PREP: 25 minutes, plus 30 minutes to marinate (optional)
COOK: 6 hours
HEAT SETTING: low

SERVES 4

2 tsp dried oregano
salt and freshly ground black pepper
2 tbsp harissa paste
large pinch saffron threads
8 chicken thighs
55g/2oz plain flour
2 tbsp olive oil
1 large onion, cut into thin wedges
2 tsp minced ginger
425ml/¾ pint hot chicken stock
400g/14fl oz canned chopped tomatoes
3 tbsp tomato purée
1 garlic bulb, halved horizontally

FOR THE GREMOLATA
small handful chopped fresh flat-leaf parsley
1 small preserved lemon, finely shredded
1 garlic clove, crushed

Mix together the oregano, half a teaspoon of black pepper, the harissa paste and the saffron threads in a large bowl. Slash the chicken thighs 3–4 times with a sharp knife, then add to the harissa mixture and coat well with the paste. If time allows, leave the meat to marinate, covered in the fridge, for 30 minutes.

Sprinkle the flour over the chicken pieces to coat them. Heat half the oil in a large frying pan over a medium-high heat and fry the chicken, in batches if necessary, until browned. Transfer to the ceramic slow cooker pot with a slotted spoon.

Add the remaining oil to the pan and fry the onion for 4–5 minutes until it is beginning to soften. Add the ginger, stock, tomatoes and tomato purée and bring to the boil, scraping up any crispy bits from the bottom of the pan. Carefully pour the mixture over the chicken pieces.

Push the 2 halves of the garlic bulb below the surface of the sauce. Cover with the lid and cook on low for 6 hours until the chicken is cooked through.

Remove the garlic and discard the papery cases. Mash the softened garlic cloves and stir back into the sauce. Season to taste.

Mix together all the gremolata ingredients and scatter over the chicken just before serving.

Riviera chicken fricassee

Tender chicken in a rich, creamy herb sauce. Look out for frozen pearl onions as they are a great timesaver: I hate peeling baby onions — life is too short.

PREP: 20 minutes
COOK: 4 hours
HEAT SETTING: high

SERVES 4

25g/1oz/2 tbsp butter
2 tbsp olive oil
1.3kg/3lb chicken, jointed
225g/8oz chestnut
    mushrooms, quartered
4 tbsp plain flour
225ml/8fl oz dry white wine
600ml/1 pint hot chicken stock
salt and freshly ground black
    pepper
juice of ½ small lemon
2 bay leaves
a few sprigs fresh thyme
85ml/3fl oz double cream
small handful chopped fresh
    tarragon leaves
125g/4½ frozen pearl
    onions
150g/5½ oz frozen peas
3 ripe tomatoes,
    skinned, deseeded
    and roughly chopped
steamed green vegetables,
    to serve
mashed potatoes, to serve

Place the butter and oil in a large frying pan and heat gently until the butter has melted. Add the chicken pieces and cook until well browned on all sides. Remove with tongs and pack the chicken into the base of the ceramic slow cooker pot.

Add the mushrooms to the frying pan and fry for 2–3 minutes until slightly coloured.

Sprinkle the flour over the mushrooms and whisk in the wine and stock, then bring to the boil and simmer until the sauce has thickened slightly.

Season well and stir in the lemon juice, bay leaves and thyme. Pour over the chicken, cover with a lid and cook on high for 3 hours.

Stir the double cream, tarragon, pearl onions, peas and tomatoes into the chicken mixture, cover with the lid and cook on high for 1 hour until the chicken is tender and cooked through.

Season to taste before serving with steamed green vegetables and mashed potatoes.

Cook's tip

To skin tomatoes: cut a cross in the top of each tomato using a sharp knife. Place the tomatoes in a large bowl and cover with boiling water, then leave to stand for 2–3 minutes. Drain and plunge the tomatoes into cold water. Tip away the water and peel them – the skin should come away easily.

Chinese chicken with pak choi and noodles

The Chinese are not known for their stews, so this is more of a soup packed full of flavour and freshness. Serve it with chopsticks for the brave and a soup spoon and fork for those who, like me, want to get the food into their mouths rather than their laps!

PREP: 25 minutes
COOK: 6½ hours
HEAT SETTING: low and high

SERVES 4

1 tbsp olive oil
4 skinless boned chicken breasts,
    cut into large strips
2 fat garlic cloves, crushed
2.5cm/1 inch fresh root ginger,
    finely chopped
2 fat red chillies, deseeded and
    thinly sliced
850ml/1½ pints hot chicken stock
3 tbsp soy sauce
3 tbsp soft brown sugar
3 tbsp dry sherry
1 tsp Chinese five-spice powder
1 large red pepper, cored,
    deseeded and cut into chunks
4–6 tbsp black bean sauce
4 heads baby pak choi,
    halved lengthways
4 dried medium egg noodle nests
2 tsp toasted sesame seeds

Heat the oil in a large frying pan over a medium-high heat and fry the chicken for 3–4 minutes, until browned all over. Stir in the garlic, ginger and most of the chillies (reserve a few for the garnish) and fry for 1 minute.

Pour over the stock and bring to the boil, scraping up any crispy bits from the bottom of the pan. Transfer the mixture to the ceramic slow cooker pot. Add the soy sauce, sugar, sherry, five-spice powder and red pepper and stir well to combine. Cover with the lid and cook on low for 6 hours until the chicken is cooked through.

Stir in the black bean sauce and push the pak choi under the sauce with a wooden spoon. Cover with the lid and cook on high for a further 30 minutes.

Meanwhile, cook the noodles according to the packet's instructions. Drain well and stir into the chicken. Scatter with the reserved red chillies and sesame seeds and serve.

Braised Italian-style squid with linguine

Squid needs to be cooked one of two ways: either very quickly, such as stir frying, or very slowly. Braising it in the slow cooker is ideal – the end result is meltingly tender pieces of squid every time.

PREP: 25 minutes
COOK: 4½ hours
HEAT SETTING: low

SERVES 4

450g/1lb small squid with
    tentacles, cleaned
1 tbsp olive oil
1 red onion, roughly chopped
400g/14oz canned chopped
    tomatoes with garlic
2 tbsp tomato purée
150ml/¼ pint white wine
55g/2oz pitted black olives
1 tsp caster sugar
finely grated rind and
    juice of 1 small
    unwaxed lemon
350g/12oz linguine
salt and freshly ground
    black pepper
small handful chopped fresh flat-
    leaf parsley (optional)

Pull the squid's tentacles out, cover and chill until ready to use. Cut the body of the squid into thick rings.

Heat the oil in a large saucepan over a medium heat and fry the red onion for 4–5 minutes, stirring occasionally, until it has softened slightly.

Add the tomatoes, tomato purée, wine, olives, sugar and lemon rind and juice and bring to the boil. Transfer the mixture to the ceramic slow cooker pot and stir in the squid rings, making sure that they are below the surface of the sauce. Cover with the lid and cook on low for 4 hours.

Push the tentacles under the surface of the sauce, cover with the lid and cook on low for a further 30 minutes.

Meanwhile, cook the linguine in a saucepan of lightly salted boiling water according to the packet's instructions. Drain well, reserving a few tablespoons of the cooking water.

Season the squid sauce to taste, adding a little extra caster sugar if necessary. Scatter over the parsley (if using). Toss with the linguine.

Cod, pepper and aubergine stew

You don't need to add a lot of liquid to this dish. If the sauce is too juicy, add a handful of toasted fresh white breadcrumbs to absorb some of the moisture — it will also add texture to the finished dish.

PREP: 15 minutes
COOK: 2 hours
HEAT SETTING: high

SERVES 4

2 tbsp olive oil
1 large onion, cut into chunks
1 aubergine, trimmed and cut
    into chunks
1 yellow pepper, cored,
    deseeded, and cut into chunks
2 fat garlic cloves, thinly sliced
1 tbsp plain flour
400g/14oz canned cherry
    tomatoes
1 tbsp tomato purée
125ml/4fl oz red wine
1 tbsp chopped fresh
    oregano leaves
600g/1lb 5oz thick-cut
    skinless cod fillets, cut into
    large pieces
salt and freshly ground
    black pepper
small handful chopped fresh flat-
    leaf parsley
crusty bread, to serve

Heat the oil in a large shallow frying pan over a medium heat and fry the onion for 5 minutes until it begins to soften. Stir in the aubergine, yellow pepper and garlic and cook for a further 2 minutes, making sure the garlic does not burn.

Sprinkle over the flour, then stir in the cherry tomatoes, tomato purée, wine and oregano and bring to the boil. Pour into the ceramic slow cooker pot. Cover with the lid and cook on high for 1 hour.

Push the fish below the surface of the sauce and season with salt and pepper. Cover with the lid and cook on high for 1 hour until the fish is cooked through.

Scatter with parsley and serve with plenty of hot crusty bread to mop up all the juices.

Spicy vegetable chilli with cornbread biscuits

A veggie chilli is a great way of using up vegetables in the fridge. Cornbread is dense, but cooked in this way it absorbs some of the juices from the sauce and is soft on the inside and crispy on the outside.

PREP: 20 minutes
COOK: 3 hours
HEAT SETTING: high

SERVES 4

1 tbsp olive oil
1 large onion, cut into wedges
2 fat garlic cloves, crushed
1 red and 1 green pepper,
    cored, deseeded and cut
    into chunks
1 large courgette, trimmed and
    cut into chunks
2 tsp hot chilli powder
2 tbsp plain flour
300ml/½ pint hot vegetable stock
2 tbsp tomato purée
400g/14oz canned chopped
    tomatoes with chilli
salt and freshly ground black
    pepper
400g/14oz canned red kidney
    beans, drained
    and rinsed
175g/6oz frozen sweetcorn

FOR THE CORNBREAD BISCUITS
250g/9oz quick-cook polenta
2 tbsp plain flour
1 heaped tsp baking powder
1 medium egg, lightly beaten
300ml/½ pint full-fat milk
125g/4½ oz mature Cheddar
    cheese, finely grated

Heat the oil in a large frying pan over a medium heat and fry the onion for 5 minutes, until it begins to soften. Add the garlic, peppers, courgette and chilli powder and fry for 3–4 minutes.

Sprinkle over the flour, then gradually stir in the vegetable stock followed by the tomato purée and chopped tomatoes and bring to the boil. Transfer the mixture to the ceramic slow cooker pot. Cover with a lid and cook on high for 2 hours.

Season with salt and pepper. Add the kidney beans and sweetcorn and stir well.

Mix together all the cornbread biscuit ingredients and spoon over the top of the vegetable chilli. Cover with the lid and cook on high for 1 hour, until the topping is set.

African vegetable and fruit stew

Fruit and vegetables have long been cooked together. Try this North African stew — the combination of sweet and savoury ingredients goes well together.

PREP: 15 minutes
COOK: 3 hours
HEAT SETTING: high

SERVES 4

2 tbsp olive oil
2 fat red chillies, deseeded
1 large red pepper, cored,
    deseeded and cut into chunks
2 tsp minced garlic
2 tsp minced ginger
1 tsp ground cumin
1 tsp ground coriander
1 tsp ground turmeric
400g/14oz canned
    chopped tomatoes
150ml/¼ pint hot
    vegetable stock
55g/2oz dried apricots, quartered
1 brown-skinned,
    orange-fleshed sweet potato,
    cut into chunks
2 tbsp mango chutney
225g/8oz fine green
    beans, trimmed
225g/8oz cashew nuts, toasted
boiled rice or wet polenta,
    to serve

Heat the oil in a large shallow frying pan and gently fry the chillies, red pepper, garlic and ginger for 1—2 minutes, stirring continuously. Add the ground spices, chopped tomatoes, stock, apricots, sweet potato, mango chutney and fine green beans and bring to the boil.

Transfer the mixture to the ceramic slow cooker pot. Cover and cook on high for 3 hours.

Grind half the cashew nuts in a food processor and stir into the stew. Scatter the remaining cashews over the stew and serve with rice or wet polenta.

Provençale vegetables with garlic croutes

It's easy to make your own garlic butter and croutes. However, if you are short of time, just buy a garlic bread baguette and slice it up.

PREP: 20 minutes
COOK: 4 hours
HEAT SETTING: high

SERVES 4

2 tbsp olive oil
1 large red onion, roughly chopped
1 small aubergine, trimmed and cut into chunks
1 large red pepper, cored, deseeded and cut into chunks
1 yellow pepper, cored, deseeded and cut into chunks
2 courgettes, trimmed and cut into chunks
4 fat garlic cloves, crushed
2 tbsp plain flour
400g/14oz canned chopped tomatoes
200ml/7fl oz hot vegetable stock
85g/3oz butter
small handful chopped fresh flat-leaf parsley
1 small baguette, thickly sliced
125g/4½ oz pitted black olives
2 tbsp pesto
salt and freshly ground black pepper

Heat the oil in a large deep frying pan and fry the onion, aubergine and peppers for 5 minutes, stirring occasionally, until they have softened slightly. Add the courgettes and three-quarters of the garlic and cook for 2 minutes.

Sprinkle over the flour and stir the chopped tomatoes and stock. Bring to the boil. Transfer the mixture to the ceramic slow cooker pot. Cover with the lid and cook on high for 3½ hours until the vegetables are tender.

Meanwhile, mash the butter, parsley and remaining garlic together and spread over the sliced bread. Chill until needed.

Stir the olives and pesto into the vegetables. Season to taste with salt and pepper. Arrange the garlic croutes on top, then cover with the lid and cook on high for a further 30 minutes.

Preheat the grill to hot. Place the ceramic slow cooker pot under the grill for 2–3 minutes until the bread starts to toast. (Keep an eye on the bread as it will cook quickly.)

Serve the Provençale vegetables with the garlic croutes.

Zesty fennel risotto with peas

It's boring standing over a bubbling pan of risotto, stirring constantly for 20–25 minutes. And although this recipe takes seven times longer, it still lovely and creamy with very little effort!

PREP: 10 minutes
COOK: 2½ hours
HEAT SETTING: low and high

SERVES 4

25g/1oz/2 tbsp butter
1 tbsp olive oil
2 fennel bulbs, trimmed and finely
    chopped
finely grated rind and
    juice of 1 unwaxed lemon
1 fat garlic clove, crushed
250g/9oz risotto rice
1.2 litres/2 pints hot
    vegetable stock
150ml/¼ pint dry white wine
175g/6oz frozen peas
salt and freshly ground black
    pepper
fresh shavings of Parmesan
    cheese, to serve
dressed salad leaves, to serve

Heat the butter and oil in a large, shallow frying pan over a medium heat and then fry the fennel, lemon rind and juice and garlic for 5 minutes, stirring occasionally, until the fennel begins to soften.

Stir in the rice and stock and bring to the boil. Transfer the mixture to the ceramic slow cooker pot. Cover with the lid and cook on low for 2 hours.

Stir in the wine and peas. Cover with the lid and cook on high for 30 minutes.

Season to taste with salt and pepper. Serve scattered with the Parmesan shavings, and with a green salad.

Roasts

Slow-roast brisket with vegetables

Brisket is a relatively cheap cut of meat and needs long, slow cooking to tenderise it. I like to leave these juices as a gravy and just mash the soft vegetables into the jus, but if you prefer, thicken the juices with a little cornflour mixed to a smooth paste with cold water.

PREP: 25 minutes
COOK: 7 hours
HEAT SETTING: high

SERVES 4–6

2 tbsp olive oil
4 red onions, quartered
4 medium carrots,
    cut into chunks
4 celery sticks (strings removed),
    cut into chunks
1.3kg/3lb beef brisket, boned
    but not rolled
salt and freshly ground black
    pepper
2 tbsp sun-dried tomato paste
1–2 tsp Dijon mustard
500ml/18fl oz hot beef stock
small handful chopped fresh
    flat-leaf parsley

Heat the oil in a large frying pan over a medium heat and fry the onions, carrots and celery for 5 minutes, until lightly browned. Transfer to the ceramic slow cooker pot using a slotted spoon.

Add the beef to the frying pan and brown well on all sides. Transfer to a plate and season with salt and pepper. Mix together the sun-dried tomato paste and mustard and spread over the beef, then arrange the meat on top of the vegetables.

Pour the stock into the frying pan and bring to the boil, scraping up any crispy bits from the bottom of the pan. Transfer to the slow cooker pot. Cover with the lid and cook on high for 7 hours or until the beef is tender and cooked through.

Lift the beef out of the slow cooker pot. Serve on a large platter with the vegetables and some of the juices spooned over, scattered with the parsley.

Best of British pot-roast beef

Beef is always a favourite, whether you are cooking for family or friends. This is a late afternoon, lazy Sunday lunch recipe: get up and put the slow cooker on; go back to bed and read the papers; go for a walk with the family, then come back once you've worked up an appetite, and your pot roast is ready.

PREP: 25 minutes
COOK: 7 hours
HEAT SETTING: high

SERVES 4

1.3kg/3lb beef topside
2 fat garlic cloves, crushed
3 tbsp vegetable oil
2 carrots, cut into chunks
2 onions, roughly chopped
4 celery sticks (strings
    removed), thickly sliced
    on the diagonal
25g/1oz/2 tbsp plain flour
600ml/1 pint hot beef stock
300ml/½ pint red wine
1 heaped tsp English mustard
1 tsp dried oregano
salt and freshly ground
    black pepper
mashed potato, to serve

Rub the beef all over with the garlic. Heat the oil in a large frying pan over a medium-high heat and fry the meat until well browned on all sides. Transfer to the ceramic slow cooker pot.

Add the carrots, onions and celery to the frying pan and fry for 5 minutes, until they begin to soften.

Sprinkle over the flour and pour over the stock and wine. Stir in the mustard and oregano and bring to the boil, scraping up any crispy bits from the bottom of the pan. Pour the mixture over the meat. Cover with the lid and cook on high for 7 hours (turning the beef halfway through cooking if you like) or until the beef is tender and cooked through.

Carefully lift the beef out of the slow cooker, place on a warm plate, slice and cover with foil.

Use a stick blender to purée the sauce. Turn the slow cooker off and strain the gravy through a sieve. Season with salt and pepper and serve spooned over the sliced beef. Serve with creamy mashed potato.

Pork tenderloin stuffed with peppers, pine nuts and ricotta

An easy recipe for entertaining. For a more unusual serving suggestion, stir
Taleggio into the sauce and toss it with your favourite type of pasta.

PREP: 30 minutes
COOK: 3½ hours
HEAT SETTING: high and low

SERVES 4

1 x large 450g/1lb pork tenderloin
12 slices pancetta
25g/1oz/2 tbsp butter
2 tbsp olive oil
1 small red onion, finely chopped
55g/2oz fresh white breadcrumbs
1 red pimento pepper, finely
    chopped
3 tbsp pine nuts, toasted
2 tbsp pesto sauce
3 tbsp ricotta cheese
salt and freshly ground
    black pepper
150ml/¼ pint dry white wine
150ml/¼ pint hot chicken stock
350g/12oz baby leaf spinach

Trim any sinew from the pork and cut the meat in half. Lay half the pork on a work surface and make a cut along the long edge, but not cutting all the way through. Open it out and lay it on a piece of cling film. Cover it with another piece of cling film and use a rolling pin to flatten the meat slightly. Repeat with the other half.

Lay 2 x 25cm/10 inch squares of cling film on a work surface and arrange the pancetta slices slightly overlapping on each, then place a piece of pork in the centre. Cover and chill.

Melt the butter and 1 tablespoon of oil in a large frying pan and fry the onion for 3–4 minutes, stirring frequently, until it softens. Remove from the heat and stir in the breadcrumbs, pimento, pine nuts, pesto and ricotta and season with salt and pepper. Divide the stuffing between the 2 pieces of pork, spooning it down the centre of each. Fold the ends of the pancetta over the short ends of the pork and then tightly roll the long sides up, as you would a Swiss roll. Secure the ends with cocktail sticks.

Heat the remaining oil in a frying pan over a medium-high heat and fry the meat for 3–4 minutes, turning frequently, until evenly browned. Transfer to the ceramic slow cooker pot.

Add the wine and stock to the frying pan and then bring to the boil, scraping up any crispy bits from the bottom of the pan. Pour the mixture into the slow cooker pot. Cover with a lid and cook on high for 1 hour. Turn down the heat to low and cook for a further 2½ hours until the meat is cooked through. Remove the meat from the juices and keep warm. Add the spinach to the hot juices and stir until it wilts. Season with salt and pepper and pile onto warm plates. Thickly slice the meat and place it on top of the spinach.

Pork fillet with prune and Armagnac filling

Parma ham can be expensive, so if you want to cut down on the number of slices you need, secure the meat in place with cocktail sticks. If you can't buy Armagnac-soaked prunes, soak ordinary ready-to-eat prunes in 1–2 tablespoons of Armagnac for 30 minutes to 1 hour.

PREP: 25 minutes
COOK: 3½ hours
HEAT SETTING: high and low

SERVES 4

large pork tenderloin (about
    450g/1lb)
8 slices Parma ham
25g/1oz/2 tbsp butter
2 tbsp olive oil
1 small onion, finely chopped
125g/4½ oz ready-to-eat
    Armagnac-soaked prunes,
    roughly chopped
25g/1oz fresh white breadcrumbs
finely grated rind and
    juice of 1 lemon
small handful chopped fresh
    flat-leaf parsley
small handful chopped fresh
    thyme leaves
salt and freshly ground
    black pepper
150ml/¼ pint dry white wine
150ml/¼ pint hot chicken stock
3 tbsp extra-thick double cream

Trim any sinew from the pork and cut the meat in half. Lay one half on a work surface and make a cut along the long edge, but not all the way through the meat. Open it out and lay it on a piece of cling film. Cover it with more cling film and use a rolling pin to flatten it. Repeat with the other half. Remove the cling film.

Lay 2 x 25cm/10 inch squares of cling film on a work surface and arrange 4 slices of Parma ham, slightly overlapping, on each, then place a piece of pork in the centre. Cover and chill.

Melt the butter and 1 tablespoon of oil in a large frying pan and fry the onion for 3–4 minutes, stirring frequently, until it softens. Remove from the heat and stir in the prunes, breadcrumbs, lemon rind, parsley and thyme and season with salt and pepper. Divide the stuffing between the 2 pieces of pork, spooning it down the centre. Fold the ends of the ham over the short ends of the pork and then tightly roll the long sides up, like a Swiss roll.

Heat the remaining oil in a frying pan over a medium–high heat and fry the meat for 3–4 minutes, shaking the pan, until evenly browned. Transfer to the ceramic slow cooker pot. Pour the wine and stock into the frying pan and bring to the boil, scraping up any crispy bits from the bottom of the pan. Pour into the slow cooker pot. Cover with the lid and cook on high for 1 hour.

Turn down the heat to low and cook for a further 2½ hours until the pork is cooked through. Remove the meat from the juices, thickly slice and arrange on serving plates. Stir the cream into the sauce and add lemon juice to taste, then spoon the sauce over the meat.

Sticky braised pork with pak choi

Belly pork definitely suits the slow cooker — the long slow cooking produces a meltingly tender piece of meat.

PREP: 25 minutes
COOK: 7¾ hours
HEAT SETTING: high

SERVES 4

1 tbsp Chinese five-spice powder
850g/1lb 14oz piece belly pork,
    rind removed
1 tbsp olive oil
1 red onion, roughly chopped
2 fat red chillies, thinly sliced
2 fat garlic cloves, crushed
2.5cm/1 inch fresh root
    ginger, grated
225ml/8fl oz orange juice,
    freshly squeezed
225ml/8fl oz hot chicken stock
4 heads pak choi
4 tbsp black bean sauce
steamed white rice, to serve

Rub the Chinese five-spice powder all over the belly pork and set aside.

Heat the oil in a large frying pan over a medium heat and fry the onion for 5 minutes, until it begins to soften and brown. Add the chillies, garlic and ginger and fry for 1 minute until fragrant.

Stir in the orange juice and stock and bring to the boil. Pour into the ceramic slow cooker pot and lay the belly pork on top. Cover with the lid and cook on high for 7 hours until the pork is cooked through.

Scatter over the pak choi, cover with the lid and cook on high for 30 minutes.

Lift the pak choi and belly pork out onto a warm plate. Stir in the black bean sauce.

Arrange the pak choi on warm serving plates. Cut the belly pork into chunks and spoon over the top. Drizzle over the sauce and serve immediately with steamed white rice.

Slow-cooked ham in cola

This dish may sound strange, but the sweet caramel qualities of the cola make it the ideal poaching liquid for a salty ham. Serve it warm or allow the ham to go cold and serve with a crisp green salad, or use to fill crusty bread rolls.

PREP: 15 minutes, plus
    overnight soaking
COOK: 6 hours
HEAT SETTING: high

SERVES 4

1kg/2lb 4oz boneless smoked
    ham, soaked overnight in
    cold water
850ml/1½ pints cola
1 star anise
5cm/2 inches fresh root ginger,
    roughly chopped
1 small onion, roughly chopped
2 celery sticks (string removed),
    roughly chopped
2 carrots, roughly chopped
1 bay leaf
2 sprigs lemon thyme
2 tbsp soft dark brown sugar
1 tbsp Dijon mustard
salt and freshly ground
    black pepper
2 tbsp runny honey

Tip away the ham-soaking water and rinse the ham in cold running water. Drain again, then pat the ham dry with kitchen paper and transfer to the ceramic slow cooker pot.

Pour the cola into a large saucepan and stir in the star anise, ginger, onion, celery, carrots, bay leaf, lemon thyme, sugar and mustard. Season with salt and pepper. Bring to the boil and then carefully pour over the ham. Cover with the lid and cook on high for 6 hours until the meat is tender and cooked through.

Preheat the grill to hot. Lift the ham out of the slow cooker pot. Remove the rind from the ham, leaving a thin layer of fat. Score the fat in a diamond pattern and drizzle over the honey. Cook the ham under the grill until the fat is bubbling and golden. If serving the ham hot, wrap it in foil to keep warm.

Meanwhile, strain the juices into a saucepan and boil rapidly until reduced by half. Season to taste and serve spooned over the sliced ham.

Provençale slow-roast lamb shanks with rustic beans

A delicious, traditional slow roast, which is perfect for enjoying on a late summer's evening.

PREP: 25 minutes
COOK: 6½ hours
HEAT SETTING: high

SERVES 4

25g/1oz/2 tbsp butter
1 tbsp olive oil
4 lamb shanks
1 large onion, sliced
1 red pepper, cored, deseeded
   and cut into chunks
1 yellow pepper, cored, deseeded
   and cut into chunks
2 tbsp plain flour
200ml/7fl oz dry white wine
450ml/¾ pint hot lamb stock
400g/14oz canned chopped
   tomatoes
1 tbsp sun-dried tomato paste
2 tbsp chopped fresh rosemary
   leaves
1 bulb garlic, halved horizontally
salt and freshly ground black
   pepper
300g/10½ oz canned flageolet
   beans, drained and rinsed
300g/10½ oz canned haricot
   or cannellini beans, drained
   and rinsed
large handful chopped fresh flat-
   leaf parsley
buttery mash or crusty bread,
   to serve

Heat the butter and oil in a large frying pan over a medium–high heat and fry the lamb shanks, turning often, until well browned on all sides. Transfer to the ceramic slow cooker pot using a slotted spoon.

Add the onion to the pan and fry for 5 minutes until it begins to soften. Add the peppers and cook for 2 minutes. Sprinkle over the flour and slowly stir in the wine and stock and bring to the boil, scraping up any crispy bits from the bottom of the pan.

Stir in the tomatoes, sun-dried tomato paste, rosemary, garlic, salt and pepper and pour the mixture over the lamb shanks. Push the garlic under the liquid. Cover with the lid and cook on high for 6 hours or until the meat is falling off the bone.

Stir in the flageolet and haricot or cannellini beans, cover with the lid and cook on high for 30 minutes. Lift the garlic out of the sauce and discard the papery skins, then mash the cloves with a fork and stir back into the sauce. Serve scattered with the fresh parsley on a pile of buttery mash, or with hot crusty bread to mop up all the juices.

Minted shoulder of lamb

Shoulder of lamb lends itself to this style of long slow cooking – the meat will fall off the bone as soon as you lift it out of the slow cooker.

PREP: 15 minutes
COOK: 7 hours
HEAT SETTING: high

SERVES 4

1 tbsp olive oil
½ shoulder of lamb
   (about 1kg/2lb 4oz)
1 large onion, roughly chopped
3 fat garlic cloves,
   roughly chopped
2 tbsp plain flour
300ml/½ pint hot lamb stock
150ml/¼ pint red wine
6 tbsp apple sauce
small handful fresh sprigs mint
salt and freshly ground
   black pepper
2 tbsp mint sauce
roast potatoes, to serve
minted peas, to serve

Heat the oil in a large frying pan over a medium-high heat and fry the lamb on each side until well browned. Carefully transfer to the ceramic slow cooker pot using 2 slotted spoons.

Add the onion to the pan and fry for 5 minutes until it begins to soften. Stir in the garlic and cook for 1 minute.

Sprinkle over the flour and gradually stir in the stock and red wine, scraping up any crispy bits from the bottom of the pan. Bring to the boil and stir in the apple sauce and a few sprigs of mint. Tip the mixture over the lamb. Cover with the lid and cook on high for 7 hours until the meat is tender and cooked through. You should be able to insert a fork into the meat and it will fall off the bone very easily.

Season to taste with salt and pepper and stir in the mint sauce.

Remove the leaves from the remaining sprigs of mint and roughly chop. Scatter over the lamb and serve with roast potatoes and minted peas.

Chicken with creamy leek and tarragon sauce

A simple Sunday roast — all you have to add are the trimmings.

PREP: 30 minutes
COOK: 5–6 hours
HEAT SETTING: high

SERVES 4 GENEROUSLY

1.3kg/3lb whole chicken
1 small lemon, halved, plus juice
  of ½ lemon (optional)
3 fat garlic cloves, crushed slightly
55g/2oz lightly salted butter
1 tbsp olive oil
1 large leek, trimmed and very
  thinly sliced
small handful fresh tarragon
  leaves, plus extra to garnish
350ml/12fl oz dry white wine
600ml/1 pint hot chicken stock
6 tbsp extra-thick double cream
salt and freshly ground black
  pepper

Put the lemon and garlic into the cavity of the chicken. Melt the butter and oil in a large frying pan over a medium-high heat and brown the chicken on all sides until nicely golden. Carefully transfer to the ceramic slow cooker pot with 2 slotted spoons.

Add the leeks to the frying pan and fry for 2–3 minutes until softened. Stir in some of the tarragon and pour over the wine and stock. Bring to the boil and pour the mixture into the ceramic slow cooker pot. Cover with the lid and cook on high for 5–6 hours.

Check to see if the chicken is cooked through after 5 hours by piercing the thickest part of the leg with a skewer. If the juices run clear it is cooked, if not, cover with the lid and cook for another hour; test again.

Carefully lift the chicken out onto a warm plate and cover with foil. Pour the sauce into a saucepan and boil rapidly until reduced by half. Stir the double cream into the sauce and use a stick blender to purée the sauce. Season with salt and pepper and add a splash of fresh lemon juice if necessary.

Carve the chicken and arrange on serving plates, then spoon over the leek and tarragon sauce.

Rolled turkey breast with ham and chestnuts

This recipe looks impressive but is very simple to make. Use vacuum-packed cooked chestnuts.

PREP: 35 minutes
COOK: 8 hours
HEAT SETTING: low

SERVES 4

500g/1lb 2oz butter-basted
    turkey breast joint
salt and freshly ground
    black pepper
4 slices Wiltshire ham
55g/2oz butter
1 onion, finely chopped
3 fat garlic cloves, crushed
2 tbsp chopped fresh thyme
    leaves
85g/3oz fresh white breadcrumbs
125g/4½oz cooked chestnuts,
    crumbled
large handful chopped fresh
    flat-leaf parsley, plus extra
    sprigs to garnish
finely grated rind and
    juice of 1 lemon
1 medium egg, lightly beaten
2 tbsp olive oil
1 large leek, trimmed and
    thinly sliced
2 tbsp plain flour
300ml/½ pint hot chicken stock
150ml/¼ pint dry white wine
2 tsp wholegrain mustard
    (optional)

Discard the skin from the turkey breast, then place it on a chopping board covered with cling film. Cover the meat with another piece of cling film and bash it with a rolling pin or meat mallet to flatten slightly. If necessary, cut a thin slice off the thickest part of the turkey breast and add it to the thinnest part, to even out the thickness. The meat, once flattened, should be about 23cm/9 inches square. Season well with salt and pepper and cover the top with the sliced ham.

Melt half the butter in a large frying pan and fry the onion for 5 minutes until it begins to soften. Stir in the garlic and continue to cook for 1 minute.

Remove from the heat and add the thyme, breadcrumbs, cooked chestnuts, flat-leaf parsley, lemon rind and juice and egg and stir until well combined. Season well and spread over the ham slices. Roll up tightly like a Swiss roll and tie at intervals with string.

Heat the oil in the frying pan over a medium–high heat and fry the turkey until browned on all sides. Transfer to the ceramic slow cooker pot using a slotted spoon.

Add the remaining butter to the frying pan and melt gently. Stir in the leek and cook for 5 minutes, stirring occasionally, until soft. Sprinkle over the flour. Pour over the stock and wine and bring to the boil, scraping up any crispy bits on the bottom of the pan. Tip into the slow cooker pot. Cover with the lid and cook on low for 8 hours until the turkey is cooked through.

Remove the turkey from the pot and cover with foil. Use a stick blender to purée the sauce until smooth. Season with salt and pepper and stir in the mustard, if you like. Serve the sauce with the thickly sliced turkey breast.

Chinese duck with star anise and plum sauce

Duck is often seen as a very fatty meat. However, once the meat has been dry fried and the rendered fat removed from the dish, it is actually quite a lean meat. Slow cooking suits duck legs and the Chinese flavours go well with its richness. Although you will never achieve crispy duck in a slow cooker, this duck dish is just as good.

PREP: 20 minutes
COOK: 5 hours
HEAT SETTING: high

SERVES 4

4 large duck legs
1 red onion, roughly chopped
2 tbsp plain flour
2 tsp Chinese five-spice powder
450ml/¾ pint hot chicken stock
1 tbsp runny honey
1 tbsp fish sauce
1 tbsp hoisin sauce
1 tbsp tomato ketchup
2 tbsp soy sauce
2 tbsp sweet chilli sauce
3 ripe plums, stones removed
    and cut into wedges
2 star anise
steamed greens, to serve
steamed white rice, to serve

Place the duck legs in a large cold frying pan and fry over a low heat until the fat starts to come out. Continue to cook until well browned and transfer to the ceramic slow cooker pot using a slotted spoon.

Tip away all but 1 tablespoon of the duck fat. Add the onion and fry for 5 minutes, until it begins to soften. Sprinkle over the flour and Chinese five-spice powder and cook for 1 minute.

Gradually add the stock and stir until thickened. Bring to the boil, scraping up any crispy bits from the bottom of the pan. Stir in the honey, fish sauce, hoisin sauce, tomato ketchup, soy sauce, sweet chilli sauce, plums and star anise. Pour the mixture over the duck legs. Cover with the lid and cook on high for 5 hours until the duck is coming away from the bone.

Adjust the seasoning to taste and serve spooned over a pile of steamed greens and rice.

Jamaican jerk chicken

This slow-cooked version of jerk chicken gets pretty close to the original – just cook the chicken first in the slow cooker, then flash it under a hot grill (or on the barbecue) to cook off the sauce and get that great chargrilled flavour. Remember to provide plenty of napkins because this chicken is finger-licking good!

PREP: 25 minutes, plus 3–4 hours
    marinating
COOK: 6 hours
HEAT SETTING: low

SERVES 4

FOR THE JERK SEASONING
2 onions, roughly chopped
3 fat red chillies, deseeded
    and roughly chopped
2 fat garlic cloves
5cm/2 inches fresh root ginger,
    finely chopped
small handful fresh thyme or
    lemon thyme leaves
½ tsp ground allspice
125ml/4fl oz cider vinegar
125ml/4fl oz light soy sauce
2 tbsp runny honey
salt and freshly ground
    black pepper

FOR THE CHICKEN
8 large skinless boneless chicken
    thighs
2 tbsp runny honey

salad, to serve

Place all the jerk seasoning ingredients into a food processor and whizz to a smooth paste. Season with salt and lots of pepper.

Slash each chicken piece 2–3 times with a sharp knife and place in a dish that is large enough to fit the pieces in a single layer. Pour over the jerk seasoning. Toss all together. Cover and leave in the fridge overnight if you have time, or for at least 3–4 hours.

Transfer the mixture to the ceramic slow cooker pot, making sure you scrape out all the marinade from the dish. Cover with the lid and cook on low for 6 hours until the chicken is tender and cooked through.

Preheat the grill to high and arrange the chicken on a foil-lined tray. Spoon over any leftover marinade from the ceramic slow cooker pot and drizzle with the extra honey. Grind over some black pepper and grill until it begins to char.

Curries & tagines

Kofta curry

I like to eat this curry cold as well as hot.

PREP: 30 minutes
COOK: 6 hours
HEAT SETTING: low

SERVES 4

FOR THE KOFTA
1 small onion, roughly chopped
1 fat garlic clove
2.5cm/1 inch fresh root ginger,
    finely chopped
1 tsp ground cumin
1 tsp ground coriander
450g/1lb lean minced beef
small handful chopped fresh
    coriander leaves
    and stems
1 tbsp vegetable oil
salt and freshly ground black
    pepper

FOR THE CURRY SAUCE
1 large onion, cut into wedges
1 tbsp vegetable oil
2 fat green chillies, deseeded and
    finely chopped
1 tbsp minced fresh ginger
5 tbsp tikka masala curry paste
400ml/14fl oz full-fat coconut milk
300ml/½ pint hot vegetable stock
1 red pepper and 1 green pepper,
    cored, deseeded and cut into
    chunks
large handful fresh coriander
    leaves and stems, roughly torn
steamed basmati rice, to serve

Place all the kofta ingredients except the oil into a food processor and season with salt and pepper. Whizz until well combined. Wet your hands and roll the mixture into 24 small balls.

Heat the oil in a large frying pan over a medium heat and fry the kofta, in batches if necessary, for 3–4 minutes, shaking the pan until they are browned all over. Transfer with a slotted spoon to the ceramic slow cooker pot.

To make the curry sauce, add the onion and the oil to the frying pan and cook for 5 minutes, stirring occasionally, until it softens slightly. Add the chillies, ginger and curry paste and fry for 1–2 minutes, stirring continuously.

Pour over the coconut milk and stock, then add the red and green peppers and bring to the boil, scraping up any crispy bits from the bottom of the pan. Tip the mixture into the ceramic slow cooker pot. Cover with the lid and cook on low for 6 hours until the meatballs are tender and cooked through.

Season to taste. Scatter with fresh coriander and serve with steamed basmati rice.

Keema curry

A traditional Gujurati-style curry made using minced lamb or beef and peas. Any leftovers can become a filling for homemade samosas. I cheat when I make samosas; I use buttered filo pastry and bake them — it's far less fiddly than deep-frying and healthier too!

PREP: 15 minutes
COOK: 7½ hours
HEAT SETTING: low and high

SERVES 4

2 tbsp olive oil
450g/1lb lean minced beef
2 onions, finely chopped
2 fat garlic cloves, crushed
1 tbsp minced fresh root ginger
4 tbsp tikka masala curry paste
400g/14oz canned
    chopped tomatoes
300ml/½ pint hot vegetable stock
1/2 tsp ground cinnamon
1 tbsp tomato purée
2 large potatoes
    (about 450g/1lb), diced
salt and freshly ground
    black pepper
175g/6oz frozen peas
steamed basmati rice, to serve

Heat the oil in a large frying pan over a medium-high heat and fry the beef, onion, garlic, ginger and curry paste for 8–10 minutes, stirring occasionally, until well browned.

Stir in the tomatoes, stock, cinnamon, tomato purée and potatoes. Bring to the boil and season with salt and pepper. Transfer the mixture to the ceramic slow cooker pot. Cover with the lid and cook on low for 7 hours until the mince is cooked through.

Stir the peas into the minced beef mixture. Cover with the lid and cook on high for 30 minutes.

Serve with the steamed basmati rice.

Beef and sweet date tagine

Sweet and sticky, this tender tagine with its fruity sauce is delicious served with lightly steamed couscous and a scattering of fresh chopped mint and coriander.

PREP: 20 minutes
COOK: 10 hours
HEAT SETTING: low

SERVES 4

1 tbsp olive oil
750g/1lb 10oz braising
    steak, cubed
1 large onion, roughly chopped
2 fat garlic cloves, sliced
2.5cm/1 inch fresh root ginger,
    finely chopped
2 tbsp plain flour
600ml/1 pint hot light beef stock
1 tsp ground cinnamon
2 large pinches saffron threads
125g/4½ oz Medjool dates,
    halved lengthways,
    stones removed
125g/4½ oz dried apricots,
    quartered
3 tbsp runny honey
small handful chopped fresh
    coriander and mint leaves
salt and freshly ground black
    pepper
55g/2oz blanched
    almonds, toasted
2 softly set hard-boiled eggs,
    shelled and quartered, to serve
steamed couscous, to serve

Heat the oil in a large frying pan and fry the beef, in batches if necessary, for about 5–6 minutes until browned on all sides. Transfer to the ceramic slow cooker pot using a slotted spoon.

Add the onion to the frying pan and fry for 5 minutes, stirring occasionally, until it softens slightly. Add the garlic and ginger and fry for 1 minute.

Sprinkle over the flour and gradually add the stock. Stir in the cinnamon, saffron, dates and dried apricots, then bring to the boil, scraping up any crispy bits from the bottom of the pan. Transfer the mixture to the ceramic slow cooker pot. Cover with the lid and cook on low for 10 hours until the beef is tender and cooked through.

Stir in the runny honey, coriander and mint and season with salt and freshly ground black pepper. Scatter with the toasted almonds and serve garnished with the softly set egg and with couscous.

Lamb rogan josh

Tender chunks of lamb in a rich spicy sauce are perfect served with plain steamed rice. I sometimes add a handful of fresh spinach and green lentils to the rice.

PREP: 20 minutes
COOK: 10 hours
HEAT SETTING: low

SERVES 4

1 tbsp olive oil
25g/1oz/2 tbsp butter
750g/1lb 10oz lamb neck
    fillet, cubed
2 onions, roughly chopped
2 fat garlic cloves, crushed
2.5cm/1 inch fresh root ginger,
    finely chopped
2 long red chillies, halved
2 tsp ground coriander
2 tsp ground cumin
1 tsp hot chilli powder
1 tsp ground turmeric
2 tbsp plain flour
400g/14oz canned chopped
    tomatoes
300ml/½ pint hot lamb stock
2 tsp garam masala
salt and freshly ground
    black pepper

TO SERVE
steamed basmati rice
1 green chilli, thinly sliced
4 tbsp natural yoghurt
    mixed with finely
    chopped coriander

Heat the oil and butter in a large frying pan over a medium-high heat and fry the lamb, in batches if necessary, for 5–6 minutes until well browned. Transfer to the ceramic slow cooker pot using a slotted spoon

Add the onion, garlic, ginger and chillies to the pan and fry for 4–5 minutes. Stir in the ground coriander, cumin, chilli powder and turmeric and cook for 1 minute.

Sprinkle over the flour and add the tomatoes, stock and garam masala. Season with salt and pepper, then bring to the boil, scraping up any crispy bits from the bottom of the pan. Tip the mixture into the ceramic slow cooker pot. Cover with the lid and cook on low for 10 hours until the lamb is tender and cooked.

Season to taste. Serve with steamed basmati rice, sprinkled with sliced green chillies and with yoghurt mixed with finely chopped coriander on the side.

Harissa lamb tagine with olives and pickled lemons

Pickled lemons add a piquant flavour to this dish. Look out for bottles of pickled lemons in the chutney and preserves section of your local supermarket. If you fancy making them yourself, check out the cook's tip.

PREP: 25 minutes
COOK: 8–9 hours
HEAT SETTING: low

SERVES 4

750g/1lb 10oz lamb neck
    fillet, cubed
1 tsp ground cumin
1 tsp sweet paprika
1 tbsp olive oil
1 large onion, roughly chopped
2 fat garlic cloves, crushed
2.5cm/1 inch fresh root
    ginger, grated
1 cinnamon stick
1 tbsp harissa paste
2 tbsp plain flour
450ml/¾ pint hot lamb stock
400g/14oz canned
    chopped tomatoes
2 tbsp tomato purée
salt and freshly ground
    black pepper
400g/14oz canned chickpeas,
    drained and rinsed
2 tbsp runny honey
125g/4½ oz pitted green olives
2 tbsp finely chopped
    pickled lemon
small handful fresh mint and
    coriander leaves
steamed couscous, to serve

In a large bowl, toss together the lamb, ground cumin and sweet paprika. Heat the oil in a large frying pan over a medium-high heat and fry the lamb, in batches if necessary, until well browned. Transfer the lamb to the ceramic slow cooker pot using a slotted spoon.

Add the onion to the frying pan and fry for 5 minutes, stirring occasionally, until it softens slightly. Add the garlic, ginger, cinnamon stick and harissa paste and fry for 1 minute.

Sprinkle over the flour. Pour over the stock, tomatoes and tomato purée and bring to the boil, scraping up any crispy bits from the bottom of the pan. Tranfer the mixture to the ceramic slow cooker pot. Season with a little salt and pepper. Cover with the lid and cook on low for 8–9 hours until the lamb is tender and cooked through.

Stir in the chickpeas and honey. Discard the cinnamon stick. Serve scattered with the green olives, pickled lemon, mint and coriander with steamed couscous.

Cook's tip

Make pickled lemons (to fill a 1 litre/1¾ pint Kilner jar): soak 10 small unwaxed lemons in warm water for 3 days. (Change the water every day; it doesn't need to be warm constantly.) Drain and quarter the lemons lengthways, not right through, leaving the stalk intact. Slightly rub 150g/5½ oz salt into the insides. Put a thin layer of any remaining salt in a dry, sterilised Kilner jar. Pack the salted lemons in. Add the juice of 8 large lemons, or enough to cover the lemons completely. Leave a little air space at the top of the jar. Leave in a cool place for at least 1 month, shaking daily.

Spicy Mexican sausage and beans

This is a one-pot 'everything in it' stew and it's sure to fill up hungry tummies. Choose good-quality sausages for the best results.

PREP: 15 minutes
COOK: 6 hours
HEAT SETTING: low

SERVES 4

1 tbsp olive oil
8 garlic and herb sausages,
    e.g. Toulouse
2 large onions, roughly chopped
6 rashers smoked streaky bacon,
    thinly sliced
2 celery sticks (strings removed)
    and finely chopped
1 large carrot, finely diced
2 fat red chillies, deseeded and
    finely chopped
3 tbsp tomato purée
350g/12oz jar tomato and chilli
    pasta sauce
2 corn on the cob, husks and
    strings removed and each cob
    cut into 6 slices
150ml/¼ pint hot chicken stock
2 tsp soft brown sugar
400g/14oz canned mixed beans,
    drained and rinsed
salt and freshly ground
    black pepper
small handful chopped fresh
    flat-leaf parsley
cornbread, to serve
lime wedges, to serve

Heat the oil in a large frying pan over a high heat and fry the sausages for 5–6 minutes until well browned. Transfer to the ceramic slow cooker pot.

Add the onions, bacon, celery and carrot to the frying pan and fry for 3–4 minutes, stirring occasionally, until the bacon is crispy and the vegetables are beginning to soften.

Stir in half the chilli and cook for 1 minute. Stir in the tomato purée, pasta sauce, corn, stock and brown sugar and bring to the boil, scraping up any crispy bits from the bottom of the pan. Pour the mixture over the sausages and stir in the beans. Cover with the lid and cook on low for 6 hours until the sausages are cooked through.

Season with salt and pepper. Scatter over the parsley and serve with warm cornbread, lime wedges and the remaining chilli, if liked.

Butter chicken

This universally popular curry should be mild and creamy. It may look difficult, but it is very simple to make. Use single cream or extra-thick double cream.

PREP: 15 minutes, plus
    30 minutes standing
COOK: 3 hours
HEAT SETTING: high

SERVES 4

1 tsp cumin seeds
1 tsp fennel seeds
1 tsp paprika
1 tsp ground turmeric
4 skinless boneless chicken
    breasts
finely grated rind and juice of 1
    unwaxed lemon
2 onions, cut into wedges
2 tsp minced ginger
2 tsp minced garlic
1 fat red chilli, deseeded and
    roughly chopped
salt and freshly ground black
    pepper
2 tbsp groundnut oil
25g/1oz/2 tbsp butter
300ml/½ pint hot chicken stock
¼ tsp ground cinnamon
4 green cardamom pods, crushed
    slightly
1 tbsp soft brown sugar
2 tbsp tomato purée
150ml/¼ pint extra-thick double
    cream
1 red onion, sliced, to serve
1 tomato, chopped, to serve
coriander leaves, to serve
black onion seeds, to serve
natural yoghurt, to serve

Put the cumin and fennel seeds in a dry frying pan and fry for 1 minute until fragrant. Tip the seeds into a pestle and mortar or spice grinder, then add the paprika and turmeric and grind to a fine powder. Tip into a large bowl.

Marinate the chicken in the lemon juice, then toss the meat in the spices. Cover and leave to marinate in the fridge for 30 minutes.

Put the onion, ginger and garlic and chilli into a food processor and whizz to a coarse paste. Add the lemon rind and season with salt and pepper.

Heat 1 tablespoon of oil and the butter in a frying pan over a medium heat and fry the chicken for 4–5 minutes, turning frequently. Add the remaining oil and the onion paste and fry for 3–4 minutes.

Add the stock, cinnamon, cardamom pods, brown sugar and tomato purée and stir well to combine. Transfer the mixture to the ceramic slow cooker pot. Cover with the lid and cook on high for 3 hours until the chicken is cooked through.

Stir in the double cream and serve scattered with a salad of sliced red onion, chopped tomatoes, coriander leaves and black onion seeds and some yoghurt.

Curried fish with lime

This rich and spicy sauce complements the tender white flakes of fish.

PREP: 10 minutes
COOK: 2½ hours
HEAT SETTING: low

SERVES 4

5 beefsteak tomatoes
1 onion, roughly chopped
2 fat garlic cloves
1 green chilli, deseeded and
    roughly chopped
2.5cm/1 inch fresh root ginger,
    roughly chopped
small handful fresh coriander
    leaves, plus extra to garnish
finely grated rind and
    juice of 2 unwaxed limes
1 tbsp coriander seeds
1 tsp fenugreek seeds
1 tsp ground turmeric
1 tbsp garam masala
1 tbsp vegetable oil
4 thick-cut cod fillets (about
    200g/7oz each)
2 tbsp plain flour
salt
steamed basmati rice, to serve

Skin the tomatoes, then roughly chop them and place them in a food processor with the onion, garlic, chilli, ginger, coriander and lime rind and juice and whizz to a fairly thick paste.

Put the coriander seeds, fenugreek, turmeric and garam masala into a dry frying pan and fry for 1 minute until fragrant, then tip the seeds into a pestle and mortar or spice grinder and grind to a fine powder.

Heat the oil in a frying pan. Dust the cod with the flour and fry it quickly on both sides for a few minutes. Transfer the cod to the ceramic slow cooker pot using a slotted spoon.

Add the ground spices to the frying pan for 20 seconds, before quickly adding the tomato paste and salt to taste. Bring to the boil and pour over the fish. Cover with the lid and cook on low for 2½ hours.

Serve with steamed basmati rice.

Thai green chicken curry

Now you can rely on your slow cooker, rather than the local takeaway, to provide an authentic Thai green curry at the end of a long day. Galangal is a type of spicy hot ginger, which adds a peppery-gingery flavour to the curry. Seek out fresh galangal in Chinese supermarkets – or look out for it in jars in the spice section of most supermarkets. If you'd like to make your own green curry paste, follow the cook's tip below.

PREP: 20 minutes
COOK: 7½ hours
HEAT SETTING: low and high

SERVES 4

1 tbsp groundnut oil
2 tbsp Thai green curry paste
2 tsp minced galangal or ginger
2 green Thai chillies,
    thinly sliced
1 onion, finely chopped
8 skinless boneless chicken thighs,
    each cut into 4 pieces
400ml/14fl oz canned full-fat
    coconut milk
150ml/¼ pint hot chicken stock
1 tbsp soft brown sugar
1 tbsp fish sauce
125g/4½ oz mangetout,
    halved lengthways
125g/4½ oz baby sweetcorn,
    halved lengthways
finely grated rind and juice of
    1 unwaxed lime and 1 lime
    cut into wedges, to serve
large handful fresh
    coriander leaves
steamed Thai fragrant rice,
    to serve

Heat the oil in a large frying pan over a medium heat and fry the curry paste for 1 minute. Stir in the galangal, chillies, onion and chicken and fry, stirring continuously, for 5 minutes.

Pour over the coconut milk and stock, then bring to the boil, scraping up any crispy bits from the bottom of the pan. Tip into the ceramic slow cooker pot. Cover with the lid and cook on low for 7 hours until the chicken is cooked through.

Stir in the brown sugar, fish sauce, mangetout, sweetcorn and lime rind and juice. Cover and cook on high for 30 minutes.

Stir in the coriander and serve with steamed rice and lime wedges.

Cook's tip

For Thai green curry paste: into a food processor put ½ teaspoon ground cumin, 1 heaped teaspoon ground coriander, 2–3 green Thai chillies, 2.5cm/1 inch fresh root galangal or ginger (finely chopped), 3 lemongrass stalks (roughly chopped), a large handful of fresh coriander leaves and stems, 6 spring onions (trimmed and roughly chopped), the rind and juice of 2 limes, 2 tablespoons of groundnut oil and 4 garlic cloves. Whizz to a paste. Use all this paste instead of 2 tablespoons of the more concentrated shop-bought paste.

Kashmiri chicken curry with almond cream

Kashmiri chilli powder is deep red and a little milder than the usual chilli powder. Don't worry if you can't find it; ordinary mild chilli powder will do just fine – unless you like things a little spicier!

PREP: 25 minutes, plus
    30 minutes standing
COOK: 6 hours
HEAT SETTING: low

SERVES 4

1 tsp cumin seeds
1 tsp fennel seeds
1 tsp Kashmiri chilli powder
1 tsp ground turmeric
8 skinless boneless chicken thighs
finely grated rind and
    juice of 1 unwaxed lemon
2 onions, cut into wedges
2 tsp minced ginger
2 tsp minced garlic
1 fat red chilli, halved lengthways
salt and freshly ground black pepper
2 tbsp groundnut oil
25g/1oz/2 tbsp butter
300ml/½ pint hot chicken stock
1 cinnamon stick
1 tbsp soft brown sugar
2 tbsp tomato purée
200g/7oz canned chopped tomatoes
100g/3½ oz flaked almonds, toasted
150ml/¼ pint extra-thick double
    cream
small handful chopped fresh coriander
    leaves and stems
1 ripe tomato, deseeded and finely
    chopped
1 small red onion, cut into wedges
1 lime, cut into wedges

Put the cumin and fennel seeds in a dry frying pan and fry for 1 minute until fragrant. Tip the seeds into a pestle and mortar or spice grinder, then add the Kashmiri chilli powder and turmeric and grind to a fine powder. Tip into a large bowl.

Marinate the chicken in the lemon juice, then toss the meat in the spices. Cover and leave to marinate in the fridge for 30 minutes.

Meanwhile, place the onions, ginger, garlic and chilli in a food processor and whizz to a coarse paste. Add the lemon rind and season with salt and pepper.

Heat 1 tablespoon of oil and the butter in a frying pan over a medium heat and fry the chicken for 4–5 minutes, turning frequently.

Add the remaining oil and the onion paste and fry for 3–4 minutes. Add the stock, cinnamon stick, brown sugar, tomato purée and tomatoes and stir well to combine. Transfer the mixture to the ceramic slow cooker pot. Cover with the lid and cook on low for 6 hours until the chicken is cooked through.

Reserve a few toasted almonds for the garnish. Place the rest in a food processor or spice grinder and whizz to fine crumbs. Stir the ground almonds into the double cream and coriander. Spoon the almond cream over the curry and scatter with the tomato, red onion and almonds. Serve with lime wedges.

Chicken tagine with figs and pomegranate

If you can, buy a whole pomegranate: roll it on a work surface to loosen the seeds before cutting it into quarters and using a teaspoon to scoop out the red seeds and juice. (Alternatively, you can buy ready-prepared pomegranate seeds in the fresh fruit section of some supermarkets.) Serve this tagine with steamed couscous, mixed with lemon rind and juice, sultanas and fresh coriander.

PREP: 20 minutes, plus
    30 minutes marinating
    (optional)
COOK: 6½ hours
HEAT SETTING: low and high

SERVES 4

salt and freshly ground black
    pepper
2 tbsp harissa paste
large pinch saffron threads
8 skinless boneless chicken thighs
55g/2oz plain flour
2 tbsp olive oil
1 large onion, cut into thin
    wedges
2 tsp minced ginger
425ml/¾ pint hot chicken stock
400g/14oz canned chopped
    tomatoes
3 tbsp tomato purée
6 fat garlic cloves, halved
    lengthways
3 tbsp runny honey
4 fresh figs, quartered
seeds from 1 pomegranate
small handful fresh
    coriander leaves
steamed couscous, to serve

Mix together half a teaspoon of pepper, the harissa paste and the saffron threads in a large bowl. Slash the chicken thighs 3–4 times with a sharp knife and coat well in the harissa paste. Cover and leave to marinate in the fridge for 30 minutes.

Sprinkle the flour over the chicken pieces to coat them. Heat 1 tablespoon of the oil in a large frying pan over a medium-high heat and fry the chicken pieces, in batches if necessary, until browned. Transfer with a slotted spoon to the ceramic slow cooker pot.

Add the remaining oil to the pan and fry the onion for 4–5 minutes, until it begins to soften. Add the ginger, stock, tomatoes, tomato purée and garlic, then bring to the boil, scraping up any crispy bits from the bottom of the pan. Pour the mixture over the chicken pieces. Cover with the lid and cook on low for 6 hours until the chicken is cooked through.

Stir in the runny honey and figs, making sure the figs are below the surface of the sauce. Cover with the lid and cook on high for 30 minutes.

Serve with couscous, scattered with the pomegranate seeds and coriander leaves.

Aromatic duck, potato and peanut curry

Duck can be quite fatty, so do remove any excess fat when cooking the duck legs but don't throw it away. Use it to roast the potatoes for your Sunday lunch.

PREP: 20 minutes
COOK: 6 hours
HEAT SETTING: high

SERVES 4

4 duck legs (about 175g/6oz each)
1 large onion, cut into wedges
2 fat green chillies, deseeded
  and finely chopped
1 tbsp minced ginger
5 tbsp mild curry paste
2 tbsp plain flour
400ml/14fl oz canned full-fat
  coconut milk
300ml/½ pint hot chicken stock
2 large potatoes, diced
salt and freshly ground black
  pepper
85g/3oz salted peanuts
1 tomato, deseeded and
  roughly chopped
large handful fresh coriander
  leaves
naan bread, to serve

Preheat a frying pan with no added oil and dry fry the duck legs, turning frequently, until the fat starts to run and the legs begin to brown all over. Transfer with a slotted spoon to the ceramic slow cooker pot.

Add the onion to the pan and cook for 5 minutes, stirring occasionally, until it softens slightly. Add the chillies, ginger and curry paste and fry for 1—2 minutes, stirring continuously.

Sprinkle over the flour and gradually add the coconut milk and stock, then bring to the boil, scraping up any crispy bits from the bottom of the pan. Transfer the mixture to the slow cooker pot and stir in the potatoes, making sure they are under the surface of the sauce. Cover with the lid and cook on high for 6 hours until the duck is tender and cooked through.

Season with salt and pepper. Scatter with peanuts, chopped tomato and coriander and serve with naan bread.

Fish molee

This lightly spiced fish curry looks great and tastes even better. Serve with spicy pickles.

PREP: 10 minutes
COOK: 1½ hours
HEAT SETTING: high

SERVES 4

1 tbsp groundnut oil
1 onion, finely chopped
1 fat garlic clove, crushed
2.5cm/1 inch fresh root ginger,
    grated or finely chopped
2 tsp ground turmeric
1 tsp hot chilli powder
1 tbsp black mustard seeds or
    black onion seeds
2 tsp ground coriander
400ml/14fl oz canned full-fat
    coconut milk
150ml/¼ pint hot vegetable stock
450g/1lb firm white fish fillets
    (i.e. cod, haddock or monkfish)
    cut into big chunks
juice of ½ lime
175g/6oz cooked tiger prawns
large handful chopped fresh
    coriander leaves
steamed basmati rice, to serve
lime wedges, to serve

Heat the oil in a large frying pan over a medium heat and fry the onion, garlic and ginger for 1 minute. Stir in the turmeric, chilli powder, mustard seeds and ground coriander and fry, stirring continuously, for 2–3 minutes.

Add the coconut milk and stock, then bring to the boil, scraping up any crispy bits from the bottom of the pan. Transfer the mixture to the ceramic slow cooker pot. Add the fish, pushing it under the sauce. Cover with the lid and cook on high for 1½ hours.

Sprinkle with lime juice (do not stir or you will break up the fish).

Heat the prawns in a pan of boiling water for 3–4 minutes. Drain and scatter over the curry with the coriander. Serve with steamed basmati rice and lime wedges to squeeze over.

Mattar paneer

Paneer is an Indian curd cheese, and is readily available from most leading supermarkets. This saucy curry just needs to be served with warm naan, to mop up the lovely rich sauce.

PREP: 10 minutes
COOK: 4 hours
HEAT SETTING: high

SERVES 4

2 tbsp olive oil
227g/8oz paneer, ripped into
    small pieces
1 large onion, halved and
    thinly sliced
2 tbsp tikka masala curry paste
450g/1lb new potatoes, quartered
1 red pepper, deseeded, cored
    and cut into chunks
1 green pepper, deseeded, cored
    and cut into chunks
400g/14oz canned chopped
    tomatoes with garlic
300ml/½ pint hot vegetable stock
225g/8oz frozen peas
salt and freshly ground
    black pepper
small handful fresh
    coriander leaves
pilau rice or naan bread, to serve

Heat the oil in a large frying pan over a medium heat and fry the paneer for 2–3 minutes until crispy and starting to brown. Transfer to the ceramic slow cooker pot using a slotted spoon.

Add the onion to the frying pan and fry for 5 minutes, stirring occasionally, until it begins to soften. Stir in the curry paste, potatoes, peppers, tomatoes and stock and bring to the boil. Pour into the slow cooker pot. Cover with the lid and cook on high for 3½ hours.

Stir in the peas. Cover with the lid and cook on high for 30 minutes. Season with salt and pepper. Scatter with the coriander and serve with naan bread or pilau rice.

Potato, chickpea and cauliflower curry

**I love this curry for all its different textures. A spoonful of mango chutney,
added at the end of the cooking time, gives a lovely tang to the sauce.**

PREP: 25 minutes
COOK: 3½ hours
HEAT SETTING: high

SERVES 4

2 tbsp groundnut oil
1 large onion, halved and
    thinly sliced
2 tbsp Madras curry paste
2 tsp minced ginger
2 tsp minced garlic
2 tsp black onion seeds
400g/14oz canned chopped
    tomatoes with chilli
300ml/½ pint hot vegetable stock
350g/12oz small cauliflower florets
350g/12oz baby
    new potatoes, quartered
150g/5½ oz baby leaf spinach
400g/14oz canned chickpeas,
    drained and rinsed
2–3 tbsp mango chutney
poppadums, to serve
lime wedges, to serve

Heat the oil in a large frying pan over a medium heat and fry the onion for 5 minutes until it begins to soften. Add the curry paste, minced ginger and garlic and onion seeds and cook for 2–3 minutes, stirring continuously.

Add the tomatoes, stock, cauliflower and potatoes, then bring to the boil, scraping up any crispy bits from the bottom of the pan. Transfer the mixture to the ceramic slow cooker pot. Cover with the lid and cook on high for 3 hours.

Stir in the spinach, chickpeas and mango chutney. Cover and cook on high for 30 minutes. Serve with some poppadums and lime wedges.

Vegetable dhansak curry

This all-in-one vegetable curry with a dal-style sauce is a sure-fire winner. The choice of vegetables is up to you, but for this cooking time softer vegetables, such as tomatoes, courgettes and peppers, are best.

PREP: 15 minutes
COOK: 3½ hours
HEAT SETTING: high

SERVES 4

175g/6oz red lentils
1 tbsp olive oil
1 large onion, finely chopped
2 red chillies, halved lengthways
small handful fresh curry
    leaves (optional)
½ tsp ground cumin
½ tsp ground coriander
½ tsp ground turmeric
2 tsp minced ginger
2 tsp minced garlic
1 tsp black onion seeds
400g/14oz canned
    chopped tomatoes
850ml/1½ pint hot
    vegetable stock
450g/1lb small cauliflower florets
salt and freshly ground black
    pepper
175g/6oz baby leaf spinach
2 large tomatoes, deseeded and
    cut into wedges
small handful fresh
    coriander leaves
naan, to serve

Place the lentils in a sieve and rinse under cold running water, then tip them into the ceramic slow cooker pot.

Heat the oil in a large frying pan over a medium heat and fry the onion, red chillies and curry leaves for 3–4 minutes. Stir in the cumin, coriander, turmeric, ginger, garlic and onion seeds and fry them for 2 minutes, stirring continuously.

Add the tomatoes and stock, then bring to the boil, scraping up any crispy bits from the bottom of the pan. Pour the mixture over the lentils.

Stir in the cauliflower, making sure it is below the surface of the sauce.

Cover with the lid and cook on high for 3½ hours.

Season with salt and pepper. Add the spinach and stir until just wilted. Scatter with the chopped tomatoes and coriander and serve with naan.

Vegetable and cashew nut biryani

Every time I cook this biryani the water content changes. Don't panic if the rice has absorbed too much water during cooking; all you need to do is add a little boiling water and separate out the rice grains with a fork.

PREP: 15 minutes
COOK: 3 hours
HEAT SETTING: low

SERVES 4

2 tbsp groundnut oil
25g/1oz/2 tbsp butter
1 onion, halved and thinly sliced
2 fat garlic cloves, crushed
1 tsp ground coriander
1 tsp ground cumin
1 tsp mild chilli powder
250g/9oz easy-cook brown rice
1 litre/1¾ pints hot
    vegetable stock
1 cinnamon stick
125g/4½ oz baby leaf spinach
3 large tomatoes, skinned,
    deseeded and chopped
salt and freshly ground black
    pepper
85g/3oz cashew nuts, toasted,
    to serve

Heat the oil and butter over a medium heat in a large frying pan and fry the onion for 5 minutes, until it begins to soften. Add the garlic, coriander, cumin and chilli and fry for 1–2 minutes, stirring continuously.

Put the rice in a sieve and rinse under cold running water. Tip it into the frying pan and add the stock and cinnamon stick. Bring to the boil, scraping up any crispy bits from the bottom of the pan. Transfer the mixture to the ceramic slow cooker pot. Cover with the lid and cook on low for 2½ hours.

Scatter over the spinach and tomatoes. Cover with the lid and cook on low for 30 minutes.

Stir well and season with salt and pepper. Serve scattered with the cashew nuts.

Thai pumpkin and red bean curry

Cut your pumpkin (or butternut squash) slightly smaller than you would normally, because in a slow cooker it can take longer to cook than meat.

PREP: 25 minutes
COOK: 8½ hours
HEAT SETTING: low and high

SERVES 4

1 tbsp groundnut oil
2 tbsp Thai red curry paste
2 tsp minced galangal or ginger
2 green Thai chillies, thinly sliced
1 onion, finely chopped
500g/1lb 2oz pumpkin or
    butternut squash, cubed
2 red peppers, cored, deseeded
    and cut into chunks
400ml/14fl oz canned full-fat
    coconut milk
150ml/¼ pint hot
    vegetable stock
1 tbsp soft brown sugar
1 tbsp fish sauce
125g/4½ oz sugar snap peas,
    halved lengthways
400g/14oz canned aduki beans,
    drained and rinsed
finely grated rind and
    juice of 1 unwaxed lime
125g/4½ oz baby leaf spinach
large handful fresh
    coriander leaves
steamed Thai fragrant rice or naan
    bread, to serve

Heat the oil in a large frying pan over a medium heat and fry the curry paste for 1 minute. Stir in the galangal, chillies, onion, pumpkin and peppers and fry, stirring occasionally, for 5 minutes.

Add the coconut milk and stock, then bring to the boil, scraping up any crispy bits from the bottom of the pan. Tip the mixture into the ceramic slow cooker pot. Cover with the lid and cook on low for 8 hours.

Stir in the brown sugar, fish sauce, sugar snap peas, aduki beans and lime rind and juice. Cover and cook on high for 30 minutes.

Stir in the spinach and coriander and serve on steamed Thai fragrant rice or naan bread.

Moroccan vegetable tagine

Harissa is a spicy condiment that gives Moroccan food a fiery kick. Native to North Africa and the Middle East, it is traditionally made from small hot peppers, cayenne, oil and garlic, pounded in a pestle and mortar with cumin seeds and mint or coriander. You can get it easily from the supermarket, however, if you want to make your own check out the cook's tip below.

PREP: 25 minutes
COOK: 6–7 hours
HEAT SETTING: low

SERVES 4

2 tbsp olive oil
1 large onion, cut into thin wedges
2 carrots, diced
450g/1lb butternut squash, cut into small chunks
1 large red pepper, deseeded, cored and diced
1 large courgette, trimmed and diced
2 tsp minced ginger
2 tsp minced garlic
400g/14oz canned chopped tomatoes
1 tbsp harissa paste
1 tsp ground turmeric
300ml/½ pint hot vegetable stock
salt and freshly ground black pepper
125g/4½ oz baby leaf spinach
400g/14oz canned chickpeas, drained and rinsed
2 tbsp runny honey
small handful chopped fresh mint and coriander leaves
steamed couscous, to serve

Heat the oil in a large frying pan over a medium heat and fry the onion for 5 minutes, until it begins to soften. Add the carrots and butternut squash and fry for 5 minutes.

Stir in the red pepper, courgette, ginger and garlic, tomatoes, harissa paste, turmeric and vegetable stock. Season with salt and pepper and bring to the boil. Tip the mixture into the ceramic slow cooker pot. Cover and cook on low for 6–7 hours until the vegetables are tender.

Stir in the spinach, chickpeas, honey and half the mint and coriander. Season to taste. Scatter with the remaining mint and coriander and then serve on top of some steamed couscous.

Cook's tip

Make your own harissa paste: put 55g/2oz dried red chillies into a bowl and pour over just enough boiling water to cover. Leave to soak for about 2 hours, until the water is cold. Drain the chillies and blend with 2 fat garlic cloves, a pinch of salt and 2 tablespoons of olive oil. Rub through a sieve and spoon into a sterilised jar. Cover the surface of the sauce with a little more olive oil to seal and store in the fridge for up to 2 months. Each time you use the harissa paste, cover it with a little oil — this will help it keep longer.

Lentil dhal

This is a great store-cupboard recipe. Whether you are serving it as an accompaniment or as the main event, it is bound to become a firm favourite in your slow-cooker repertoire.

PREP: 10 minutes
COOK: 3 hours
HEAT SETTING: high

SERVES 6–8
as an accompaniment or
4 as a main dish

225g/8oz red lentils
1 tbsp olive oil
1 large onion, finely chopped
small handful fresh curry leaves
    (optional)
½ tsp ground cumin
½ tsp ground coriander
½ tsp ground turmeric
2 tsp minced ginger
2 tsp minced garlic
400g/14oz canned
    chopped tomatoes
600ml/1 pint hot vegetable stock
175g/6oz baby leaf spinach

Place the lentils in a sieve and rinse under cold running water, then tip into the ceramic slow cooker pot.

Heat the oil in a large frying pan over a medium heat and fry the onion and curry leaves, if using, for 3–4 minutes. Stir in the cumin, coriander, turmeric, ginger and garlic and fry for 2 minutes, stirring continuously.

Add the tomatoes and stock, then bring to the boil, scraping up any crispy bits from the bottom of the pan. Pour the mixture over the lentils. Cover with the lid and cook on high for 3 hours.

Add the spinach and stir until it wilts.

Side
dishes

Mediterranean stuffed peppers

Couscous is a great ingredient to keep in your store cupboard. These peppers are lovely served with all sorts of dishes, including a roast chicken — they look so enticing on the plate as well as tasting wonderful.

PREP: 15 minutes
COOK: 4 hours
HEAT SETTING: low

SERVES 4
as an accompaniment or
2 as a light supper

1 large red pepper
1 large yellow pepper
salt and freshly ground
    black pepper
85g/3oz couscous
225ml/8fl oz hot vegetable stock
2 tbsp pine nuts, toasted
55g/2oz raisins
125g/4½ oz red cherry
    tomatoes, halved
125g/4½ oz marinated feta
    cubes, drained, plus 1 tbsp
    of the oil
2 tbsp green pesto
a few fresh basil leaves

Cut each pepper in half lengthways through the stalk. Remove the core and seeds, keeping the green stalk in place. Season with salt and pepper.

Put the couscous in a bowl and pour over 75ml/2½fl oz of the hot stock. Cover with cling film and set aside for 5–7 minutes, until all the stock has been absorbed.

Remove the cling film and fluff up the couscous with a fork. Add the pine nuts, raisins, cherry tomatoes, feta and pesto. Stir well to combine and season with salt and pepper. Divide the mixture between the peppers.

Brush the oil (from the feta) inside the base of the ceramic slow cooker pot and arrange the peppers, filling side up, in the pot.

Pour the remaining stock around the peppers and cook on low for 4 hours. Remove from the slow cooker with a slotted spoon and serve scattered with fresh basil.

Braised fennel, olive and Parmesan gratin

Fennel has a slightly aniseedy flavour, which goes very well with grilled fish. It is also wonderful served with stews and casseroles to cut through their richness. Celery is a good substitute and can be cooked in the same way.

PREP: 15 minutes
COOK: 5 hours
HEAT SETTING: high

SERVES 4

4 medium fennel bulbs
grated rind and juice of 1
   unwaxed lemon
1 tbsp olive oil
400g/14oz canned
   chopped tomatoes
2 tbsp tomato purée
2 tbsp golden caster sugar
12 pitted black olives
25g/1oz Parmesan
   cheese, grated
crusty bread, to serve

Trim the feathery coarse tops from the fennel and slice off any discoloured parts from its base, then thinly slice it and toss it immediately in the lemon juice. Scatter it into the base of the ceramic slow cooker pot.

Mix together the lemon rind, olive oil, tomatoes, tomato purée, sugar and olives and tip them over the fennel. Cover with the lid and cook on high for 5 hours.

Scatter over the Parmesan and allow to melt with the heat from the dish. Serve with crusty bread to mop up all the juices.

Baked aubergines with tomatoes

It's less common nowadays for recipes to call for salting aubergines, to drain away their bitter juice. However, in this recipe salting helps to release some of the aubergines' water content and prevents this dish from being too watery. The sun-dried tomato purée adds a robust flavour.

PREP: 15 minutes, plus
    20 minutes salting
COOK: 5 hours
HEAT SETTING: high

SERVES 4

2 medium aubergines
2 tbsp table salt
3 tbsp olive oil
freshly ground black pepper
190g/6½ oz sun-dried
    tomato paste
4 large beefsteak tomatoes
150ml/¼ pint hot vegetable stock
25g/1oz Parmesan cheese,
    finely grated
small handful of fresh basil leaves,
    to serve

Trim the aubergines and thinly slice them lengthways. Layer them in a colander, sprinkling salt between each layer. Stand the colander on a plate and then set aside for 20 minutes to remove any bitter juices.

Rinse off the salt under cold running water and pat the aubergine slices dry using kitchen paper. Brush the slices on both sides with the olive oil and season with pepper.

Preheat a griddle pan until smoking hot and chargrill the aubergine in batches, until charred on both sides.

Spread half the sun-dried tomato paste over the base of the ceramic slow cooker pot. Layer the aubergine and tomatoes on top. Mix together the remaining sun-dried tomato paste and the stock and pour over the aubergines and tomatoes. Cover with the lid and cook on high for 5 hours.

Preheat the grill to high. Turn off the slow cooker and remove the ceramic slow cooker pot. Sprinkle over the Parmesan cheese and grill for 2 minutes until golden. Serve scattered with fresh basil leaves.

Aubergine and chickpea pilaff

Whether you serve this pilaff as a vegetarian supper or as a side dish, it hits the spot. Make sure you buy easy-cook rice as it is simpler to cook in a slow cooker. There's no need to salt the aubergine first for this recipe.

PREP: 20 minutes
COOK: 3½ hours
HEAT SETTING: low

SERVES 6
as an accompaniment or
4 as a light supper

3 tbsp olive oil
1 large onion, finely chopped
1 medium aubergine, trimmed
    and cut into small cubes
2 tsp minced garlic
2 tsp minced ginger
1 cinnamon stick
2 green cardamom pods,
    lightly crushed
2 bay leaves
large pinch saffron threads
1 litre/1¾ pints hot
    vegetable stock
200g/7oz easy-cook rice
85g/3oz dried apricots, quartered
25g/1oz raisins
1 tbsp tomato purée
400g/14oz canned
    chickpeas, drained
150g/5½oz cherry tomatoes
salt and freshly ground
    black pepper
small handful of fresh coriander
    leaves, torn

Heat 1 tablespoon of the oil in a large frying pan over a medium heat and fry the onion for 5 minutes, until soft and beginning to colour. Add the remaining oil and stir in the aubergine, garlic, ginger, cinnamon stick, cardamom and bay and fry for 4–5 minutes, until the aubergine is soft and fragrant.

Add the saffron and stock and scrape up any crispy bits from the bottom of the pan. Stir in the rice, apricots, raisins, tomato purée, chickpeas and cherry tomatoes and bring to the boil.

Transfer the mixture to the ceramic slow cooker pot. Cover with the lid and cook on low for 3–3½ hours, until the rice is tender and the stock has been absorbed.

Remove the cinnamon stick. Stir well and season with salt and pepper. Serve scattered with some fresh coriander.

Puy lentil braise

Puy lentils are hearty and satisfying. Serve this dish with grilled fish or, even better, rich venison sausages.

PREP: 15 minutes
COOK: 7 hours
HEAT SETTING: low and high

SERVES 4

1 tbsp olive
1 large red onion, cut into
    thin wedges
1 red pepper, cored, deseeded
    and cut into chunks
1 yellow or orange pepper, cored,
    deseeded and cut into chunks
2 fat garlic cloves, crushed
2 tbsp fresh thyme leaves
1 bay leaf
400g/14oz canned
    chopped tomatoes
300ml/½ pint hot vegetable stock
150ml/¼ pint red wine
3 tbsp tomato purée
1 tbsp golden caster sugar
225g/8oz Puy lentils
150g/5½ oz baby plum tomatoes
small handful chopped fresh
    flat-leaf parsley
salt and freshly ground
    black pepper

Heat the oil in a large frying pan over a medium heat and fry the onion and peppers for 5–6 minutes, until softened.

Stir in the garlic, thyme, bay leaf, tomatoes, stock, red wine, tomato purée, sugar and lentils and bring to the boil. Transfer the mixture into the ceramic slow cooker pot. Cover with the lid and cook on low for 6 hours.

Stir in the plum tomatoes and scatter over the parsley. Turn the slow cooker to high. Cover with the lid and cook for 1 hour. Season with salt and pepper.

Garlicky sweet potato and onion gratin

Serve this with gamey stews. The gratin's sweetness will be a sharp contrast to the richness of the stew.

PREP: 15 minutes
COOK: 5 hours
HEAT SETTING:high

SERVES 4

25g/1oz/2 tbsp butter, softened
1 large red onion, thinly sliced
1 tsp dried sage
2 fat garlic cloves, crushed
450g/1lb brown-skinned, orange-fleshed sweet potatoes, thinly sliced
450g/1lb waxy potatoes, thinly sliced
salt and pepper
450ml/16fl oz hot vegetable stock
55g/2oz Gruyère cheese, finely grated

Brush the butter around the base and sides of the ceramic slow cooker pot.

Mix together the onion, sage and garlic. Layer the onion mixture with the sweet potatoes and waxy potatoes, seasoning with salt and pepper as you go.

Pour over the stock and scatter with the cheese. Cover with the lid and cook on high for 5 hours, until the potatoes are tender.

Preheat the grill to high. Grill for 3–4 minutes until golden.

Baked onions with sun-dried tomatoes

Need something to perk up your Sunday roast? Look no further. These are the onions for you — packed full of Mediterranean flavours.

PREP: 20 minutes
COOK: 3 hours
HEAT SETTING: high

SERVES 4

2 large Spanish onions
2 tbsp sun-dried tomato paste
55g/2oz toasted dried
    breadcrumbs
6 semi-dried sun-blush
    tomatoes in oil, halved,
    plus 2 tbsp of their oil
1 garlic clove, crushed
4 large basil leaves, shredded,
    plus extra to garnish
1 medium egg, beaten
salt and freshly ground
    black pepper
150ml/¼ pint hot light
    chicken stock
a few fresh basil leaves

Bring a large pan of lightly salted water to the boil. Add the whole onions in their skins, with the roots intact, and boil for 10 minutes. Drain and allow to cool.

When the onions are cool, trim off the roots and peel. Cut the onions in half horizontally, then use a teaspoon to scoop out enough of the centre of each to leave a shell at least 3 onion layers thick. Finely chop the scooped-out onion and place in a bowl.

Add the tomato paste, breadcrumbs, sun-blush tomatoes plus 1 tablespoon of their oil, garlic, basil and egg to the bowl. Season with salt and pepper and mix thoroughly. Spoon the stuffing back into the onions and pack down well.

Brush the remaining oil inside the base of the ceramic slow cooker pot and arrange the onions on top. Pour the stock around the onions and cover with the lid. Cook on high for 3 hours, until the onions are meltingly tender but still retain their shape. Serve scattered with fresh basil.

Cook's tip

If you like, brown the cooked onions under a hot grill, and the remaining stock can be quickly reduced in a saucepan to make a jus to drizzle over them.

Braised celery with orange and cardamom

Ground cardamom is available from most Indian shops and some supermarkets. If you do have difficulty buying it, just buy green cardamom pods. Crush the pods and remove the black seeds, then grind them in a pestle and mortar and sieve to give cardamom powder.

PREP: 10 minutes
COOK: 5 hours
HEAT SETTING: high

SERVES 4

2 celery hearts
grated rind and juice of
    1 unwaxed orange
2 tbsp golden caster sugar
1 tsp ground cardamom
1 tbsp sweet sherry
400g/14oz canned
    chopped tomatoes
55g/2oz fresh white breadcrumbs
small handful chopped fresh
    flat-leaf parsley
25g/1oz/2 tbsp butter, melted
salt and freshly ground black
    pepper

Trim off any discoloured celery and cut each celery heart in half lengthways, then place into the base of the ceramic slow cooker pot.

Mix together the orange juice, golden caster sugar, ground cardamom, sweet sherry and chopped tomatoes and pour over the top. Cover with the lid and cook on high for 5 hours until the celery is tender.

Turn off the slow cooker. Drain off the juices into a saucepan and boil rapidly for 3–4 minutes to reduce the sauce to a syrup. Season to taste and pour back over the celery.

Preheat the grill to high. Mix together the breadcrumbs, orange rind, parsley and melted butter. Scatter over the celery and grill until crisp and golden. Serve scattered with fresh parsley.

Candied sweet potatoes

This very American dish, traditionally served with the Thanksgiving roast, is well worth a try. Make sure you choose brown-skinned sweet potatoes as they have soft orange flesh when cooked. Sweet potatoes do have a very sweet flavour, so adding more sweetness with the stem ginger may seem mad but it definitely works!

PREP: 10 minutes
COOK: 4 hours
HEAT SETTING: high

SERVES 4

750g/1lb 10oz brown-skinned, orange-fleshed sweet potatoes, cut into chunks
100ml/3½fl oz orange juice, freshly squeezed
2 tbsp stem ginger syrup
1 ball stem ginger, shredded
½ tsp ground cinnamon
freshly ground black pepper
55g/2oz chopped walnuts
snipped fresh chives

Place the sweet potatoes into the ceramic slow cooker pot.

Combine the orange juice, ginger syrup, stem ginger, cinnamon and freshly ground black pepper in a small saucepan. Heat gently until warmed through and pour over the sweet potatoes. Cover with the lid and cook on high for 4 hours, until the sweet potato is tender.

Serve scattered with the walnuts and chives.

Creamy celeriac and potato dauphinoise

This is rich and satisfying, so a little goes a long way. If you have a mandoline, dig it out from your cupboard and use it to slice the potatoes, onion and celeriac.

PREP: 15–20 minutes
COOK: 2½ hours
HEAT SETTING: high

SERVES 4

1 celeriac (about 750g/1lb 10oz)
salt and freshly ground black
    pepper
650g/1lb 7oz King Edward
    potatoes, very thickly sliced
55g/2oz butter, softened
1 tbsp olive oil
2 large Spanish onions,
    thinly sliced
1 tsp dried thyme
small handful chopped fresh
    flat-leaf parsley
125g/4½ oz mature Cheddar
    cheese, finely grated
150ml/¼ pint hot vegetable stock
2 tbsp wholegrain mustard
150ml/¼ pint double cream

Peel the celeriac, working quickly as the flesh will brown fast. Quarter and cut into thin slices. Bring a large pan of lightly salted water to the boil and add the celeriac and potatoes and boil for 10 minutes. Drain well.

Meanwhile, rub some of the butter around the base and sides of the ceramic slow cooker pot, then heat the remaining butter and oil in a large frying pan. Fry the onion and thyme for 5–7 minutes, until the onion begins to turn golden brown. Stir in the flat-leaf parsley.

Layer the potato and celeriac, onion mixture and cheese in the ceramic slow cooker pot, seasoning with pepper between each layer and finishing with a layer of potatoes and celeriac and then cheese. Pour over the stock. Cover with the lid and cook on high for 2 hours.

Mix together the mustard and cream. Remove the lid and pour over the cream mixture. Cover with the lid and cook on high for a further 30 minutes.

Preheat the grill to hot. If you wish to, transfer the dauphinoise to a heatproof serving dish. Place the ceramic slow cooker pot or dish under the grill for 2–3 minutes, until golden brown.

Desserts
& cakes

Red fruit compote with lemon cream

Sponge fingers are the ideal biscuits to soak up all the lovely red fruit juice from the berries. This easy dessert is a modern take on a simple trifle.

PREP: 20 minutes
COOK: 1 hour
HEAT SETTING: high

SERVES 4

4 red plums, halved,
    stones removed and cut
    into chunks
125g/4½ oz strawberries, hulled
    and quartered
125g/4½ oz cherries, pitted
55g/2oz golden caster sugar
finely grated rind and
    juice of 3 unwaxed limes
150ml/¼ pint double cream
2 tbsp lemon curd
8 sponge fingers
4 lime wedges

Scatter the plums, strawberries and cherries into the base of the ceramic slow cooker pot. Sprinkle over the sugar and lime rind, then pour over the lime juice and 125ml/4fl oz boiling water. Cover with the lid and cook on high for 1 hour until the fruit is tender.

Lightly whip the double cream, add the lemon curd and stir once or twice until the curd is rippled through the cream.

Break up the sponge fingers and divide them between 4 glasses. Spoon over the fruit compote and top with the lemon cream mixture. Decorate each glass with a lime wedge.

Cardamom rice pudding with honey-roasted figs

This is pure comfort food and, although you do not get the traditional rice pudding crust, this version is totally satisfying.

PREP: 10 minutes
COOK: 2½ hours
HEAT SETTING: low

SERVES 4

175g/6oz pudding rice
finely grated rind and
    juice of 1 unwaxed lemon
55g/2oz sultanas
2 green cardamom pods,
    lightly crushed
400ml/14fl oz canned
    condensed milk

FOR THE FIGS
3 fresh figs, quartered
2 tbsp runny honey

Place the rice into a sieve and rinse well under cold running water, then tip into the ceramic slow cooker pot. Stir in the lemon rind and juice, sultanas, cardamom pods and pour over 1 litre/1¾ pints boiling water. Cover with the lid and cook on low for 2½ hours.

Preheat the grill to hot 10 minutes before the end of the cooking time. Arrange the figs on a baking tray and drizzle with the runny honey. Grill until just beginning to char.

Stir the condensed milk into the rice pudding and serve with the figs.

Maple, apricot and pecan nut sponge pudding

This looks impressive when it's turned out and the maple syrup dribbles down the sides of the pudding. Serve it steaming hot with lashings of creamy custard or single cream.

PREP: 15 minutes
COOK: 5 hours
HEAT SETTING: high

SERVES 6

175g/6oz butter, softened, plus
    extra for greasing
55g/2oz pecan halves
55g/2oz dried apricots
3 tbsp maple syrup
150g/5½oz light
    muscovado sugar
3 medium eggs, lightly beaten
finely grated rind and
    juice of 1 unwaxed orange
225g/8oz self-raising flour, sifted
single cream, to serve

Lightly grease a 1.4 litre/2½ pint pudding basin. Scatter the pecan nuts and dried apricots into the base of the pudding basin and drizzle over the maple syrup.

In a large bowl, beat together the butter and muscovado sugar until light and creamy. Add the beaten eggs a little at a time. Fold in the orange rind and flour, until well combined, then add enough orange juice to produce a soft dropping consistency. Spoon the sponge mixture into the basin and level the surface.

Butter a square of greaseproof paper. Fold a pleat into the centre of the paper and place it buttered side down over the top of the pudding basin. Cover the pudding basin with a pleated piece of foil and secure with a string handle.

Place the pudding basin into the ceramic slow cooker pot and pour in enough boiling water to come halfway up the side of the basin. Cover with the lid and cook on high for 5 hours.

Carefully lift the pudding out of the slow cooker and discard the foil and greaseproof paper. Turn out onto a serving plate and serve with single cream.

Red wine and port-poached pears

These pears are so versatile: serve them warm with ice cream or chocolate sauce or cold as part of your cheese board at the end of the meal, or chop the pears into chunks and add to a crisp green salad to serve with rich cured meats, such as duck or smoked chicken.

PREP: 15 minutes
COOK: 4 hours
HEAT SETTING: high

SERVES 6

6 ripe pears
450ml/¾ pint red wine
finely grated rind and
    juice of 2 unwaxed oranges
200g/7oz caster sugar
1 cinnamon stick
150ml/¼ pint ruby port

Peel the pears, leaving the stalks intact if possible, and arrange them in the ceramic slow cooker pot.

Pour over the red wine and 350ml/12fl oz boiling water. Add the orange rind and juice, sugar and cinnamon stick. Crumple a large square of greaseproof paper and place under cold running water, then open it out slightly and use to cover the pears (this will help keep them under the surface of the liquid). Cover with the lid and cook on high for 4 hours.

Carefully lift the pears out of the syrup and transfer to a large bowl.

Pour the red wine mixture into a saucepan and add the port. Boil rapidly for 5–6 minutes or until reduced by half. Pour the syrup over the pears and, if necessary, chill until ready to serve.

Rich chocolate espresso cups

Smooth, dark, rich chocolate pots served with crisp biscuits is the ultimate way to complete an evening meal.

PREP: 15 minutes, plus 3 hours chilling
COOK: 3½ hours
HEAT SETTING: low

SERVES 4

400ml/14fl oz full-fat milk
50ml/2fl oz espresso
300ml/½ pint double cream
225g/8oz 70% dark chocolate, broken into pieces
2 medium eggs, plus 3 egg yolks
85g/3oz caster sugar
large pinch ground cinnamon
2 amaretti biscuits, crushed

Place the milk, espresso, half the double cream and 200g/7oz dark chocolate into a saucepan and heat gently, stirring, until the chocolate has melted and the ingredients are well combined.

Whisk together the eggs and yolks, sugar and cinnamon. Gradually whisk in the chocolate mixture and pour into 4 x 250ml/9fl oz ramekins or heatproof dishes. Cover the dishes tightly with foil and place into the ceramic slow cooker pot. Pour in enough boiling water to come halfway up the sides of the dishes. Cover with the lid and cook on low for 3½ hours, until just set.

Lift the dishes out of the slow cooker and chill for at least 3 hours, or overnight if you have time.

When you are ready to serve, finely chop the remaining chocolate. Whip the remaining cream and scatter over the chopped chocolate and crushed amaretti. Stir once or twice to swirl them through the cream. Spoon the cream on top of the chocolate pots and then serve immediately.

Desserts & cakes 221

Chocolate brownie cake slices

This cakey brownie slice will hit the spot with an afternoon cup of tea.
Unfortunately you don't get the characteristic crusty brownie top, so
dust them heavily with cocoa powder before serving.

PREP: 20 minutes,
    plus cooling
COOK: 2 hours
HEAT SETTING: high

MAKES 6 SLICES

55g/2oz 70% dark chocolate,
    broken into pieces
25g/1oz/2 tbsp unsalted
    butter, softened
55g/2oz caster sugar
2 tsp golden syrup
1 large egg, lightly beaten
pinch salt
1 tsp vanilla extract
25ml/1fl oz/2 tbsp warm
    full-fat milk
25g/1oz/2 tbsp plain flour, sifted
¼ tsp baking powder
25g/1oz/3 tbsp walnut pieces
25g/1oz/2 tbsp raisins
1 tbsp cocoa powder, sifted

Line the base and sides of a 900g/2lb loaf tin with greaseproof paper (make sure your tin will fit into the ceramic slow cooker pot).

Melt the chocolate in a bowl set over a pan of simmering water (but not touching the water).

Meanwhile, in a separate bowl, cream together the butter and sugar. Beat in the golden syrup, egg, salt, vanilla and milk until smooth. Beat in the melted chocolate and fold in the flour, baking powder, walnuts and raisins. Pour into the prepared tin.

Cover the top of the tin tightly with foil and put it into the ceramic slow cooker pot. Pour in enough boiling water to come halfway up the sides of the tin. Cover with the lid and cook on high for 2 hours.

Carefully remove the tin from the slow cooker and allow the cake to cool completely in the tin.

Remove the cake from the tin and discard the lining paper. Dust the top with cocoa powder and slice into 6 pieces.

Fruit cake with a pecan crust

A rich moist fruit cake topped with pecan nuts and sugar, which give this modern slow cooker cake a traditional twist.

PREP: 25 minutes, plus
    30 minutes soaking
COOK: 5 hours
HEAT SETTING: high

SERVES 8

55g/2oz butter, softened, plus
    extra for greasing
5 tbsp hot Earl Grey tea
225g/8oz dried mixed fruit
125g/4½ oz light muscovado
    sugar
1 large egg, lightly beaten
150g/5½ oz wholemeal
    self-raising flour, sifted
pinch salt
½ tsp mixed spice
55g/2oz glacé cherries, washed
55g/2oz whole pecan nut halves
1 tbsp demerara sugar

Grease and line the base and sides of a 15cm/6 inch soufflé dish or fixed-base cake tin that will fit easily inside your ceramic slow cooker pot with greaseproof paper, so that the paper comes 2.5cm/1 inch above the rim of the dish or tin.

Pour the hot tea over the mixed fruit in a bowl and set aside for at least 30 minutes to soak.

Cream the butter and muscovado sugar together and beat in the egg a little at a time.

Drain the mixed fruit, if necessary, to get rid of any excess tea.

Fold the flour, salt, mixed spice, mixed fruit and glacé cherries into the egg mixture and combine well. Spoon the mixture into the prepared dish or tin and level the surface. Arrange the pecan halves on the surface of the cake. Scatter over the demerara sugar.

Place the cake in the ceramic slow cooker pot with a large strip of folded foil underneath the dish and hanging over the rim of the pot – this will help you lift the dish out of the slow cooker easily. Cover with the lid and cook on high for 5 hours.

Lift the cake out of the slow cooker and allow to cool completely in the tin. Remove the cake and discard the lining paper. Wrap the cake in foil and store in a cool place for up to 1 week.

Sticky chocolate self-saucing pudding with vanilla cream

There's no doubt about it, this pudding is rich and stodgy and just oozing with dark chocolate sauce.

PREP: 20 minutes
COOK: 2½–3 hours
HEAT SETTING: high

SERVES 6

125g/4½ oz unsalted
   butter, softened
175ml/6fl oz full-fat milk
200g/7oz caster sugar
1 tsp vanilla extract
225g/8oz self-raising flour
4 tbsp cocoa powder
1 medium egg, lightly beaten
225g/8oz light muscovado sugar

FOR THE VANILLA CREAM
1 vanilla pod, split
200ml/7fl oz crème fraiche

Use 15g/½ oz/1 tbsp butter to coat the inside of the ceramic slow cooker pot.

Melt the remaining butter in a large saucepan, then remove it from the heat and stir in the milk, caster sugar and vanilla extract.

Sift over the self-raising flour with half the cocoa powder and add the egg. Mix until well combined and pour into the ceramic slow cooker pot.

Mix together the muscovado sugar and remaining cocoa powder and sprinkle over the pudding mixture.

Gently pour 600ml/1 pint boiling water over the brown sugar mixture. Cover with the lid and cook on high for 2½–3 hours, until the pudding has set.

For the vanilla cream, scrape the seeds from the vanilla pod and stir them into the crème fraiche. Serve the vanilla cream with the warm saucy chocolate pudding.

Ginger crème caramels

Sweet and gingery, these little puddings are sure to become a family favourite. I always keep stem ginger in my store cupboard – it's great for adding to curries, tagines, soups and custard. When you have used all the stem ginger balls, don't throw away the syrup. It is wonderful when used to sweeten lemon or fruit tea.

PREP: 20 minutes, plus 3 hours
    chilling
COOK: 3 hours
HEAT SETTING: low

SERVES 4

25g/1oz/2 tbsp unsalted butter,
    softened
125g/4½ oz caster sugar
1 ball stem ginger, finely chopped,
    plus 2 tbsp syrup from the jar
400ml/14fl oz can condensed milk
125ml/4fl oz full-fat milk
2 medium eggs, plus 3 egg yolks

Grease 4 x 250ml/9fl oz individual metal pudding basins, ramekins or teacups with the butter.

Place the sugar into a small saucepan and pour over 125ml/4fl oz water. Bring to the boil and then boil rapidly for 5 minutes until the syrup starts to turn golden brown. Carefully divide the caramel between the basins. Tilt the basins until the base and sides are coated in the caramel (watch out if you are using metal basins as the outsides will become hot).

Scatter the chopped ginger into the base of each basin.

Pour the condensed milk, full-fat milk and half the stem ginger syrup into a saucepan and heat gently. Whisk together the eggs and egg yolks in a large bowl, then pour in the warm milk mixture. Strain the mixture through a sieve back into the saucepan.

Divide the milk mixture between the basins and cover the tops tightly with foil. Place the basins into the ceramic slow cooker pot. Pour in enough boiling water to come halfway up the sides of the basins and cook on low for 3 hours until the custards have only just set – they will still have a wobbly centre (this will set on cooling).

Carefully remove the basins from the slow cooker and chill for at least 3 hours, or overnight if you have time.

To release the puddings from the basins, gently ease the edge of the custards away from the sides with your fingertips. Then dip each basin into hot water for 10–20 seconds, turn upside down onto a plate and shake gently until you hear the pudding release itself onto the plate.

Ginger iced parkin

This moist ginger cake works well in the slow cooker. Slice the stem ginger really thinly for the topping to make the cake easier to slice.

PREP: 15 minutes, plus cooling
COOK: 3½ hours
HEAT SETTING: high

SERVES 8

4 balls stem ginger, very
    thinly sliced
125g/4½oz lightly salted butter
125g/4½oz dark muscovado
    sugar
125g/4½oz golden syrup
200g/7oz wholemeal
    self-raising flour
½ tsp bicarbonate of soda
2 tsp ground ginger
2 medium eggs, lightly beaten
100ml/3½fl oz full-fat milk
85g/3oz icing sugar
2 tbsp stem ginger syrup

Line the base and sides of a 900g/2lb loaf tin with greaseproof paper (make sure your tin will fit into the ceramic slow cooker pot). Arrange the stem ginger slices on the base of the loaf tin.

Put the butter, sugar and golden syrup into a large saucepan and heat gently, stirring occasionally, until the butter has melted and the sugar has dissolved. Remove from the heat and leave to stand for 10 minutes.

Stir the flour, bicarbonate of soda, ground ginger, eggs and milk into the golden syrup mixture and beat until well combined. Carefully pour the mixture into the prepared tin, trying not to disturb the stem ginger.

Cover the top of the tin really loosely with cling film. Place the tin into the ceramic slow cooker pot and pour in enough boiling water to come halfway up the sides of the tin. Cover with the lid and cook on high for 3½ hours or until a skewer inserted into the centre of the cake comes out clean.

Carefully remove the tin from the slow cooker and let the cake cool completely in the tin. Remove the cake from the tin and discard the lining paper.

Mix together the icing sugar and stem ginger syrup to a smooth icing and drizzle over the cake. Allow to set.

Christmas pudding

This recipe is not my own. It comes from Edith, my sister's mother-in-law. We eat this every Christmas without fail. We all love it! If you are looking for a light, fruity Christmas pudding, then this is the recipe for you. Serve with brandy butter, cinnamon-spiced custard or single cream.

PREP: 10 minutes
COOK: 5 hours
HEAT SETTING: high

SERVES 6–8

a little butter, for greasing
150g/5½ oz self-raising flour
85g/3oz fresh white breadcrumbs
150g/5½ oz suet
225g/8oz caster sugar
250ml/9fl oz full-fat milk
150g/5½ oz raisins
150g/5½ oz currants
1 level tsp bicarbonate of soda
2 tsp mixed spice
1 medium egg, lightly beaten
1 tbsp icing sugar, sifted

Grease a 1.4 litre/2½ pint pudding basin that will fit easily into your ceramic slow cooker pot with plenty of butter. Mix together all the remaining ingredients until well combined and spoon into the prepared basin. Cover the basin tightly with greaseproof paper and foil (both with a pleat in the centre) and tie a string handle over the top so that you can easily remove the pudding from the slow cooker.

Lower the basin into the ceramic slow cooker pot. Pour in enough boiling water to come two-thirds up the side of the basin. Cover with the lid and cook on high for 5 hours.

Carefully lift out of the slow cooker and discard the greaseproof paper and foil. Turn out onto a serving plate and lightly dust with icing sugar.

Marmalade bread-and-butter pudding

Make sure that you find a 1.2 litre/2 pint soufflé or ovenproof dish that fits into your ceramic slow cooker pot — you need to have a space about 2.5cm/1 inch all the way around the dish and it should be at least 7.5cm/3 inches deep. This recipe uses the slow cooker as a bain-marie to obtain that lovely just-set texture.

PREP: 20 minutes, plus
    20 minutes soaking
COOK: 4 hours
HEAT SETTING: low

SERVES 4

100g/3½ oz butter, softened
6 medium slices day-old bread,
    crusts removed
4 tbsp fine shred marmalade
4 egg yolks
55g/2oz caster sugar
150ml/¼ pint double cream
300ml/½ pint full-fat milk
1 tsp vanilla extract
25g/1oz/2 tbsp icing sugar
strawberries, to serve
single cream, to serve

Grease a 1.2 litre/2 pint soufflé or ovenproof dish (see introduction) with 25g/1oz/2 tbsp butter. Use the remaining butter to spread over the slices of bread. Spread the marmalade over 3 slices of bread and make into sandwiches with the remaining bread. Cut into quarters and arrange, slightly overlapping, in the buttered dish.

Beat together the egg yolks and sugar in a medium bowl.

Pour the double cream and milk into a saucepan and warm gently until just below boiling. Pour the milk over the egg mixture and whisk until well combined. Whisk in the vanilla extract. Strain through a sieve and pour over the bread. Leave to stand for 20 minutes in order to allow some of the liquid to be absorbed.

Put a metal cookie cutter or upturned saucer into the base of the ceramic slow cooker pot and lay a large folded piece of foil on top of the dish, wide enough and long enough to help you lift the dish out of the slow cooker. Lower the dish into the ceramic slow cooker pot so that it sits comfortably on the cutter or saucer. Cover with the lid and cook on low for 4 hours, until the custard has set.

Preheat the grill to hot. Carefully lift the dish out of the slow cooker pot using the foil strip to help you. Remove and discard the foil. Dust the icing sugar over the pudding and grill until lightly browned (keep an eye on the pudding — it will brown quickly). Serve with strawberries and single cream.

Lemon drizzle poppy seed loaf

One slice will not be enough of this moreish lemon drizzle cake — it will have you coming back for more... and more...

PREP: 20 minutes, plus
    cooling time
COOK: 2½ hours
HEAT SETTING: high

MAKES A 900g/2lb LOAF

175g/6oz unsalted butter,
    softened
250g/9oz caster sugar
3 medium eggs
175g/6oz self-raising flour,
    sifted
2 tbsp poppy seeds
3 unwaxed lemons

Line the base and sides of a 900g/2lb loaf tin with greaseproof paper (make sure your tin will fit into the ceramic slow cooker pot).

In a large bowl, beat together the butter and 175g/6oz sugar until creamy. Beat in the eggs, flour, poppy seeds and finely grated zest of 2 lemons, until the mixture is well combined. Pour into the prepared loaf tin and cover the top loosely with foil.

Put an upturned saucer or metal cookie cutter into the base of the ceramic slow cooker pot. Place the loaf tin on top. Pour in enough boiling water to come halfway up the sides of the tin. Cover and cook on high for 2½ hours or until a skewer inserted into the centre of the cake comes out clean.

Remove the tin from the slow cooker. Discard the foil and carefully slice off any cake that has risen above the top of the tin (you can eat that bit!). While the cake is still hot, remove it from the tin and discard the lining paper.

Meanwhile, use a potato or vegetable peeler to pare thin slivers of lemon rind from the remaining lemon and then cut away any white pith. Shred the lemon rind very thinly and put it in a small saucepan with the remaining sugar and the juice from the 3 lemons, then heat gently until the sugar has dissolved. Serve with the syrup and lemon rind and leave to cool completely.

Preserves

Piquant piccalilli

This is the perfect accompaniment to Slow-cooked Ham in Cola (see page 134) if you are serving it cold, with a crisp green salad. Using the slow cooker to cook the vegetables is great as you avoid that acrid vinegar smell that you normally get when cooking this on the stove.

PREP: 30 minutes, plus
    overnight salting
COOK: 1 hour
HEAT SETTING: high

MAKES 4 X 400g/14oz
JAM JARS

125g/4½oz fine green beans,
    trimmed and cut into 2.5cm/
    1 inch pieces
1 large red pepper, cored,
    deseeded and finely diced
225g/8oz small cauliflower florets
250g/9oz cucumber, diced
125g/4½oz table salt
227g/8oz jar cocktail onions,
    drained and rinsed
1 tsp ground turmeric
2 tsp English mustard powder
½ tsp ground ginger
85g/3oz granulated sugar
450ml/¾ pint distilled
    malt vinegar
4 tsp cornflour

Place the green beans, red pepper, cauliflower and cucumber in a colander and put the colander over a large bowl. Sprinkle with the salt, cover and leave to stand overnight.

Rinse the vegetables very well under cold running water to remove the salt. Tip them into the ceramic slow cooker pot with the cocktail onions. Add the turmeric, mustard powder, ginger, sugar and vinegar and stir until combined. Cover with the lid and cook on high for 1 hour.

Meanwhile, sterilise 4 x 400g/14oz clean jars by washing them in hot, soapy water and then drying them in an oven preheated to 140°C/275°F/Gas mark 1 for 12–15 minutes. Spoon the vegetables into the warm jars.

Switch off the slow cooker. Lift out the ceramic slow cooker pot and tip the juices into a saucepan. Mix the cornflour with a little cold water to form a smooth paste and then drizzle this into the piccalilli sauce mixture. Heat gently for 2–3 minutes, until the sauce has thickened.

Pour over the vegetables to cover, then cover each jar with a waxed paper disc and seal tightly with a lid. When cold, store in a cool dark place for up to 2 months. Once opened, store in the fridge; it will keep for 2–3 weeks.

Fruit-bowl chutney

This is a great way of using up any fruit in your fruit bowl. If including bananas, only use one per batch and chop it very finely. Perfect with crusty bread.

PREP: 20 minutes
COOK: 6 hours
HEAT SETTING: high

MAKES 3 X 400g/14oz JARS

450g/1lb tomatoes, skinned and
    roughly chopped
2 red onions, finely chopped
2 eating apples, peeled, cored
    and roughly chopped
2 peaches or nectarines, stones
    removed, and roughly
    chopped
125g/4½ oz dried apricots,
    finely chopped
85g/3oz sultanas or raisins
150ml/¼ pint distilled
    malt vinegar
2 tsp wholegrain mustard
4 tbsp soft dark brown sugar
4 fat garlic cloves, crushed
1 star anise
1 tsp salt

Place all the ingredients in the ceramic slow cooker pot and stir well. Cover with the lid and cook on high for 6 hours, stirring once or twice during cooking.

Place a ladleful of the chutney in a food processor and whizz until smooth. Stir it back into the chutney.

Meanwhile, sterilise 3 x 400g/14oz clean Kilner or jam jars by washing them in hot, soapy water and then drying them in an oven preheated to 140°C/275°F/Gas mark 1 for 12–15 minutes. Spoon the hot chutney into warm jars, cover each with a waxed disc and seal tightly with a lid. When cool, store in a cool dark place for 2 months before eating. Once opened, store in the fridge; it will keep for 2–3 weeks.

Tomato and chilli jam

Spice up your cheese and crackers, your bacon sarnie or even your scrambled eggs with this great-tasting homemade jam. Once opened, store it in the fridge and use within 3 weeks.

PREP: 20 minutes, plus 4 hours
soaking
COOK: 6 hours
HEAT SETTING: high

MAKES 2 X 400g/14oz JARS

225g/8oz dried apricots,
quartered
4 fat garlic cloves, halved
1 large red onion, roughly
chopped
5cm/2 inches fresh root ginger,
finely chopped
3 small red chillies (not Thai),
deseeded and roughly
chopped
150ml/¼ pint cider vinegar or
seasoned rice wine vinegar
450g/1lb ripe tomatoes,
roughly chopped
2 tbsp tomato purée
2 tsp vegetable bouillon powder
3 tbsp soft dark brown sugar

Mix the apricots, garlic, onion, ginger, chillies and vinegar in a large bowl, cover and soak for at least 4 hours.

Add the remaining ingredients and blend with a stick blender to a coarse purée. Pour the mixture into the ceramic slow cooker pot. Cover with the lid and cook on high for 6 hours.

Meanwhile, sterilise 2 x 400g/14oz clean Kilner or jam jars by washing them in hot, soapy water and then drying them in an oven preheated to 140°C/275°F/ Gas mark 1 for 12–15 minutes. Spoon the hot jam into the warm jars. Cover each with a waxed paper disc and seal tightly with a lid. When cold, store in a cool dark place for up to 3 months. Once opened, store in the fridge; it will keep for 2–3 weeks.

Versatile barbecue sauce

**No *al fresco* dining table should be without this sauce.
It's great with bangers, burgers and barbecued meats.**

PREP: 15 minutes, plus
    4 hours soaking
COOK: 6 hours
HEAT SETTING: high

MAKES 1.5 LITRES/2¾ PINTS

125g/4½ oz dried apricots,
    roughly chopped
55g/2oz sultanas
55g/2oz raisins
5 tbsp sherry
150ml/¼ pint red wine vinegar
450g/1lb ripe tomatoes, skinned
    and roughly chopped
2 onions, finely chopped
4 garlic cloves, crushed
finely grated rind and juice
    of 1 unwaxed orange
1 tsp table salt
1 tsp freshly ground
    black pepper
2 tbsp tomato purée
3 tbsp soft dark brown sugar
1 tbsp Dijon mustard
2 splashes Worcestershire sauce

Place the apricots, sultanas and raisins in a bowl. Pour over the sherry and red wine vinegar. Cover and soak for at least 4 hours.

Pour the dried fruit and soaking liquid into a food processor, add all the remaining ingredients and whizz. Tip the mixture into the ceramic slow cooker pot. Cover with the lid and cook on high for 6 hours.

Meanwhile, sterilise clean jars by washing them in hot, soapy water and then drying them in an oven preheated to 140°C/275°F/Gas mark 1 for 12–15 minutes. Pass the mixture through a sieve for a completely smooth sauce, or leave chunky if you prefer. Spoon the hot sauce into warm jars or bottles and seal tightly with the lids. When cold, store in a cool dark place for up to 3 months. Once opened, store in the fridge; it will keep for 2–3 weeks.

Tangy three-fruit curd

This tangy fruit curd will have a runnier texture than a bought thickened curd. It's great with hot buttered toast or homemade scones.

PREP: 15 minutes, plus
    15 minutes cooling
COOK: 4 hours
HEAT SETTING: low

MAKES 2 X 400g/14oz JARS

125g/4½ oz unsalted butter
400g/14oz golden caster sugar
finely grated rind and juice of
    2 unwaxed lemons
grated rind and juice of
    1 large unwaxed orange
grated rind and juice of
    1 large unwaxed lime
4 medium eggs, plus 2 egg yolks

Melt the butter in a heavy-based saucepan over a medium heat. Stir in the sugar and the rind and juice from the lemons, orange and lime. Heat gently, stirring, until all the sugar has dissolved. Leave to cool for 10–15 minutes.

Find a pudding basin that will easily fit into the base of your ceramic slow cooker pot and pour in the mixture.

Whisk together the eggs and yolks, then strain them through a sieve into another bowl. Whisk the strained eggs with a fork into the lemony mixture. Cover the basin tightly with foil and tie with a string handle to make it easy to lift. Place the bowl into the ceramic slow cooker pot and pour in enough boiling water to come halfway up the side of the pudding basin. Cover with the slow cooker lid and cook on low for 4 hours.

Meanwhile, sterilise 4 x 400g/14oz clean Kilner or jam jars by washing them in hot, soapy water and then drying them in an oven preheated to 140°C/275°F/ Gas mark 1 for 12–15 minutes. Spoon the hot mixture into the warm jars, cover each with a waxed disc and seal tightly with the lids. Allow to cool completely. Store in the fridge and use within 1 month. Once opened it will keep for 2–3 weeks.

Strawberry, apple and lavender jam

Although this jam looks very wet when it has finished cooking, it will thicken as it cools. Spoon over scones with thickly whipped double cream and fresh berries.

PREP: 15 minutes
COOK: 3 hours
HEAT SETTING: high

MAKES 4 X 400g/14oz JARS

900g/2lb cooking apples, peeled, cored and roughly chopped
450g/1lb granulated sugar
grated rind and juice of
   1 small unwaxed lemon
225g/8oz strawberries, sliced
1 sprig lavender (unsprayed)

Place all the ingredients into the ceramic slow cooker pot and stir well. Cover with the lid and cook on high for 3 hours, stirring once or twice during cooking. (At the end of the cooking all the fruit will be floating on the top of the sugar syrup.)

Discard the sprig of lavender. Blend the mixture together using a stick blender.

Meanwhile, sterilise 4 x 400g/14oz clean Kilner or jam jars by washing them in hot, soapy water and then drying them in an oven preheated to 140°C/275°F/ Gas mark 1 for 12–15 minutes. Spoon the hot jam into the warm jars, cover each with a waxed disc and seal tightly with the lid. Allow to cool completely. This jam does not keep as well as traditionally made jam, so it needs to be stored in the fridge. Use within 6 weeks. Once opened it will keep for 2–3 weeks.

Index